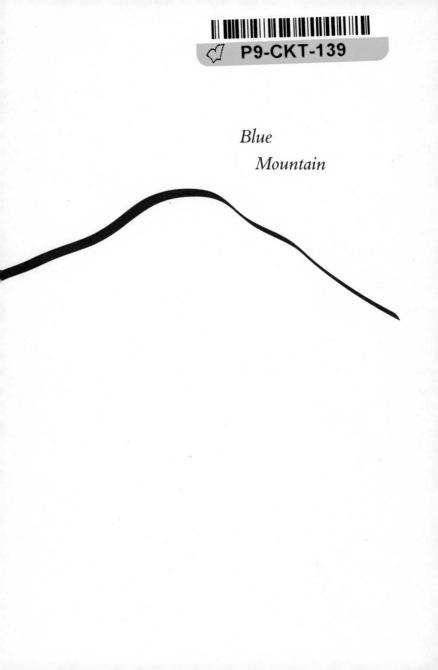

Blue
Mountain

BLUE MOUNTAIN

A Spiritual Anthology
Celebrating the Earth

F. Lynne Bachleda

Menasha Ridge Press

Copyright © 2000 by F. Lynne Bachleda
All rights reserved
Published by Menasha Ridge Press
Distributed by The Globe Pequot Press
First edition, first printing

Cover design and photograph by Grant Tatum
Interior book design by B. Williams & Associates
Icons created by Hopkins Design Group, Inc.

Cataloging-in-Publication Data is available
from The Library of Congress.
ISBN: 0-89732-311-4

Permissions are gratefully acknowledged, and listed on page 193.

Menasha Ridge Press
P.O. Box 43673
Birmingham, AL 35243
(205) 322-0439
www.menasharidge.com

Big Blue Mountain Spirit,
The home made of blue clouds . . .
I am grateful for that way of goodness there.

Apache chant

———◆———

First there is the forest and inside the forest the
clearing and inside the clearing the cabin and
inside the cabin the mother and inside the mother
the child and inside the child the mountain.

Jeannette Winterson
Gut Symmetries

———◆———

I believe in God, only I spell it Nature.

Frank Lloyd Wright

With love to my parents, Fleeta and Al.
You taught me the power of the smallest seed
and the glory of the shooting star. By your
example, I learned that fur and feathers are
family, too. You have my eternal gratitude.

CONTENTS

INTRODUCTION

One to One

The faces of the earth are many; the Spirit of the Earth is One. Appreciating the selections in *Blue Mountain,* therefore, does not require a history of globe-spanning adventures witnessing the various magisterial splendors of our terrestrial home. No matter where we may have literally traveled, these words can help us to imagine and to undertake the larger emotional and spiritual journey. The pilgrimage destination is as exotic or familiar, as arduous or accessible as you care to make it, but it is a destination found outdoors.

Thoreau declared, "In wildness is the preservation of the world." I believe that in wildness is the preservation of the soul. More than ever, we need to seek out a renewal of our spirits from the Creator's ultimate manifest source. Nature alone has always been regarded by all peoples as an authentic cache of the Holy.

John Burroughs, one of America's seminal nature writers, commented on the great availability of companionship that Nature offers. Her door is always open, her treasures, and often her terrors, on display. Nature unfailingly responds to our overtures in surprising and expected ways that can comfort, startle, amuse, charm, and challenge us.

As always it seems, the miracle comes not when sought, but when least expected, and it only comes with practice. To know and be known by Nature requires nothing more and nothing less than spending time with her as we would a cherished friend—listening, looking, revealing, laughing, crying, and praying together.

The journey with Nature we have before us, then, is like her seasons, a cyclical process of ongoing renewal. The arc of this book offers but one way to think about the spiritual journey with the Divine Earth. I hope it encourages you to spend time with Her, to find your way from desire and need ultimately through to hope and resolve.

Sit on the step at sun's rise and drink your coffee. Circuit the backyard, the far pasture, or the beach to see the night's offerings. Take a walk in the city park with a friendly dog, or a friend who loves dogs. Sit by the lake with a lover, enchanted by reflected possibilities. Hike the paths that whisper a thrill. Languish in the grassy field, sunshine's magnetic sponge. Sit by the camp fire and merge into dreamtime. Bike sloshing creeks and fragrant pine paths. Paddle the river's roar or float on its glass. Trek to the summit's Marian blue vista, breathe, and wind down. If you do any of these things and perceive a connection with the Spirit, this book is for you.

What Is Blue Mountain?

At this juncture to know not, or to believe not, in the ecological crisis that surrounds us is to claim an ignorance that is neither bliss, nor blessed. This collection, however, is not a cry of alarm or a funeral dirge. By comparison, *Blue Mountain* is a quest and a celebration. The song I sought to sing here was to help all of us fall in love again, to help all of us reacquaint ourselves with our most ancient of friends for the most holy of days. My belief is that in this loving, in this genuine relationship, we will rise to cherish and to protect our beloved. And, oh, how she longs to hold us, and to be held, too!

Of course, all the old connections that tie us profoundly to the earth are in place. Like pagans on a pilgrimage to the holy ground that will be Chartres, we have risen in the dark to witness the sun's rise on Easter. We have hauled in greenery at light's low tide and return. We have sent our children, if they are lucky, outdoors to play. And children who have been awakened to these oldest rhythms never lose the texture of those days of ice cascades that sing winter's song, or the fresh lap of salt and shimmer shifting at the edge of the sea.

The passionate path home to the earth winds and turns in our hearts as long as we live, but we must walk it to keep the weeds down; to see the fragile breathing ribs of the tiny lizard; to witness Linda Hogan's "great turning over of the world" as flesh reenters the Source; to find perennial cheer in the gold of the finch; and to release our spirits to swell during a desperately needed downpour.

I have no doubt we are all connected directly to this most ancient, most global main line of worship, to the white light before the rainbow refractions of the faiths splintered it. To seek this old grace goes so deeply it rings of cliché: it's as natural as breathing, as right as rain, as intangible as a cloud, as palpable as a flower, as tender as a breeze, and as miraculous as the sun's sure rise.

How to Use This Book

What is the *Blue Mountain* itinerary? Encompassing and nonexistent. Always free to roam randomly and intuitively, perhaps you will find oracular wisdom here. By design, however, these chapters move through a revolving sequence of relationship to the Divine. In seeking a fresh structure for this work, I looked at my own spiritual life. What I observed was a familiar cycle of stages named in the chapter headings. In short, I organized this work with the everyday hero in mind. Emptied by life's demands and difficulties to the starting point of desire and need, this hero must return to the Source to be filled again with hope and resolve, to be restored and readied to re-enter life, only to be emptied again. Nature is the Source, and this hero is you.

Blue Mountain has seven chapters or guideposts for a spiritual journey. The path of seven stages originates with a longing that might also feel like loneliness — a *need or desire* to reconnect with the vitality and possibilities offered by nature. Once the summons is answered and the modest or grand journey outdoors is undertaken, simple observation generates a sense of *marveling and adoration* at the variation, beauty, and meaning abundant in the natural world. This appreciation cannot help but lead to feelings of *comprehension and joy* at the richness that is ours in nature. As we realize that we are not just chess pieces dropped on top of the board, but rather integral, equal elements of this grand scheme, our sense of separation dissolves. A knowledge of *connection and unity* with all of God's creation evolves. *Redemption* from our own smaller world gains foothold, feeding a freeing gift of *grace* that can expand into our hearts and minds and even bodies. So comforted are we now, the self's boundaries are expanded to *recognition and compassion* for all living beings. With an enlarged, reconnected, graceful, and compassionate sense of self, we can return to the part of our lives lived "indoors," with a reaffirmed sense of *hope and resolve* for our selves and our world.

Off the Path

Solomon, the author of Ecclesiastes, was right. There is a time under heaven for everything, so there is also a time for veering off the marked path, wandering away on your own. *Blue Mountain* has maximum flexibility—use the given sequence or invent your own. The symbol set offers an alternative path that will guide you to entries for seasons, elements, and particular wisdom tradition passages.

Purely random seekers will also be rewarded.

In the Near, Here and Now

Near where I live, and I'll bet near you, too, the earth is losing ground. Oh, not in the eternal way, not in the way of eons and millennia and shifts so mighty the mind cannot hold them. No, we shall not destroy her bedrock, I think. But you know what I mean. Easy access to pure nature is a road closing fast. Even in the center an 800-acre small town park, the roar of Harleys penetrate my hour of prayer.

So I say visit the wildest places you can, while you can. As Thomas Berry writes, "The dream of the earth. Where else can we go for the guidance needed for the task that is before us." The earth is destined to show us regeneration, trembling, majesty, cruelty, usefulness, awe, the everlasting, and the long and deep of it all. Witness these and find the surer footing, the truer balance so many of us seem to seek.

You'll see my calling for this is, in the Biblical sense, "as old as the hills." The refrain echoes to all of us for good reason. It is because there are answers in the hills, and so much more. When the near-sightedness of greed and the blindness of parochialism threatens the earth, I literally go to the earth for the wisdom, the ways, the tools to help her, to help me. Nature's intelligence soars past our unused minds. I ask for that wisdom to come into me. I cannot name it, do not know it, but I do know it exists. Like sorcerers of old, if we ask, it is given.

Journeys Prior to Jerusalem

Blue Mountain explores the timeless ways, the ways we are everlastingly united. There is a broader, more important bridge of joy out of doors for our best, borderless selves. Together, forever, we can stand on cavernous, craggy cliffs at the edge of the sea, or bow low and reverentially to smell a rose. The music of the earth, of which we are players and instruments, never conductors, connects us with the ancients, with the all, with Dylan Thomas' "force that through the green fuse drives the flower."

Everywhere we stand together, then, we are standing on sacred ground, on the *Blue Mountain*. Our excitement sparks at a shooting star. We realize the relief and caress of breeze. We really see the silver sheen on water. Even when the earth's elemental forces knock us down, back, or even out, bestowing a proper sense of proportion in their wake, we stand here together partaking of our profound common green communion. May it always be so.

Benediction

Fellow travelers, then, may the cadenced wisdom of the forest, the steadfast life of the sun, the soaring heart of the birds, the power of this earth that climbs from destruction to create again, may these inform and rise up through you as you stand on your own *Blue Mountain*.

THE SYMBOL SET

Because Menasha Ridge Press and I hope you will take this book outdoors, we thought it would also be useful to provide a thumb index symbol set to help you find entries that pertain to the essential elements of your surroundings. For just a few examples, here all animals and trees are "Earth;" stars are "Fire;" sky and sound are "Air;" and "Water" finds its myriad expressions. Imperfectly, we have also expanded this system to include icons for the world's wisdom traditions that, if known, reflect the tradition of the writer, or the sensibility of the selection itself. We hope these tools will be useful to you as we seek an essential common global ethic for our work here together.

Earth

Water

Air

Fire

Spring

Summer

Autumn

Winter

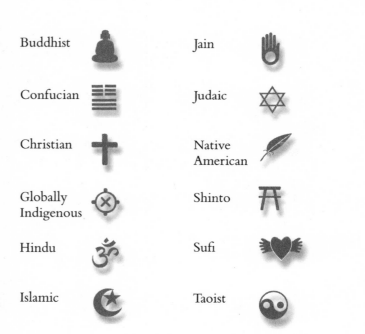

Buddhist		Jain	
Confucian		Judaic	
Christian		Native American	
Globally Indigenous		Shinto	
Hindu		Sufi	
Islamic		Taoist	

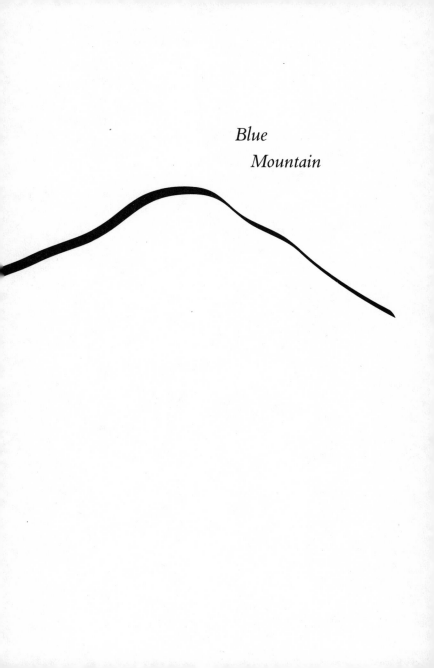

Blue
Mountain

ONE

FROM DESIRE AND NEED

Where we begin when we seek Nature

Desire and need arise from separation and can produce a simple want to go outdoors to register the sky's offerings of moisture, light, and temperature. More deeply felt is a need to imbibe the grand elixir common to life on earth. Simply, your empty cup calls to you for running out, and hence over.

All journeys have a secret destination of which the traveler is unaware.

Martin Buber
Tales of the Hasidim

——•——

I only went out for a walk, and finally concluded to stay out till sundown, for going out, I found, was really going in.

John Muir
Journal

——•——

The best remedy for those who are afraid, lonely,
or unhappy is to go outside, somewhere where they can be quite alone with the heavens, nature and God. Because only then does one feel that all is as it should be and that God wishes to see people happy, amidst the simple beauty of nature.

Anne Frank
*The Diary of Anne Frank:
The Critical Edition*

The moon is a friend for the lonesome to talk with.

Carl Sandburg
"Moonlight and Maggots,"
The Complete Poems of Carl Sandburg

It is often true that the best things we do in some strange way take place within us long before we come to the ground itself. The physical domain of the country had its counterpart in me. The trails I made led outward into the hills and swamps, but they led inward also. And from the study of things underfoot, and from reading and thinking, came a kind of exploration, myself and the land. In time the two became one in my mind. With the gathering force of an essential thing realizing itself out of early ground, I faced in myself a passionate and tenacious longing—to put away thought forever, and all the trouble it brings, all but the nearest desire, direct and searching. To take the trail and not look back. Whether on foot, on snowshoes or by sled, into the summer hills and their late freezing shadows— a high blaze, a runner track in the snow would show where I had gone. Let the rest of mankind find me if it could.

John Haines
The Stars, The Snow, The Fire

"Blackbird"

Blackbird singing in the dead of night
Take these broken wings and learn to fly
All your life
You were only waiting for this moment to arise.

Blackbird singing in the dead of night
Take these sunken eyes and learn to see
All your life
You were only waiting for this moment to be free.

John Lennon & Paul McCartney

And I said, Oh that I had wings like a dove!
for then I would fly away, and be at rest.
Lo, then would I wander far off, and remain in the
    wilderness.

King David
Psalm 55:6–7

"Measure Me, Sky"

Sky, be my depth;
Wind, be my width and my height;
World, my heart's span:
Loneliness, wings for my flight!

Lenora Speyer

Rest is not idleness, and to lie sometimes on the grass
on a summer day listening to the murmur of the water,
or watching the clouds float across the sky, is hardly a
waste of time.

John Lubbock

Often when I walk out from my house into the hills surrounding it, I discover after twenty minutes or so that I have taken the house with me, have taken the unanswered letters and telephone calls, the windows that need caulking, the slights I suffered last week, the things I should have said but didn't, the things I plan to say next week but probably won't. My feet have been taking a walk without me. Every step has been clouded by the metronome beat of "yes, no, yes, no." Words like ground squirrel, cinquefoil, osprey, and dove flit across my consciousness in response to beings that appear, but I don't see them. It doesn't matter whether the ground I'm walking over is planted alfalfa or wild knapweed, whether the trees are virgin or second growth. If I am not aware of them, not conscious of their consciousness, nature doesn't exist for me, though I may be walking in Tierra del Fuego.

Dan Gerber
"Walking in Tierra del Fuego,"
*Sacred Trusts: Essays on
Stewardship & Responsibility*

A person wielding a fifty-ton digger in search of coal will learn quite different lessons from one who wields a pair of binoculars in search of warblers. . . . Generally we hear what our ears have been prepared for, and if we do not go seeking divinity we are not likely to find it.

Scott Russell Sanders
"Tokens of Mystery,"
Secrets of the Universe

"The Peace of Wild Things"

When despair for the world grows in me
and I wake in the night at the least sound
in fear of what my life and my children's lives may be,
I go and lie down where the wood drake
rests in his beauty on the water, and the great heron feeds.
I come into the peace of wild things
who do not tax their lives with forethought
of grief. I come into the presence of still water.
And I feel above me the day-blind stars
waiting with their light. For a time
I rest in the grace of the world, and am free.

Wendell Berry
The Selected Poems of Wendell Berry

Beyond the walls and solid roofs of houses is the out-doors. It is always on the doorstep. The sky, serene, or piled with white, slow-moving clouds, or full of wind and purple storm, is always overhead . . . You visit the woods or the mountains or the sea on your vacation. You loaf along trout streams, or in red autumn woods with a gun in your hands for an excuse, or chase golf balls over green hills, or sail on the bay and get be-calmed and do not care. For the pleasure of living out-doors you are willing to have your eyes smart from the smoke of the camp fire, and to be wet and cold, and to fight mosquitoes and flies. You like the feel of it, and you wait for that sudden sense of romance everywhere which is the touch of something big and simple and beautiful. It is always beyond the walls . . . .

> Edna Brush Perkins
> "The Feel of the Outdoors,"
> *The White Heart of Mojave:*
> *An Adventure with the Outdoors of the Desert*

The walk you take to-day through the fields and woods, or along the river-bank, is the walk you should take to-morrow, and next day, and the next. What you miss once, you will hit upon next time. The happenings are at intervals and are irregular. The play of Nature has no fixed programme. If she is not at home to-day, or is in a non-committal mood, call to-morrow, or next week.

John Burroughs
"New Gleanings in Old Fields,"
Field & Study

A man in Anaktuvuk Pass, in response to a question about what he did when he visited a new place, said to me, "I listen." That's all. I listen, he meant, to what the land is saying. I walk around in it and strain my senses in appreciation of it for a long time before I, myself, ever speak a word. Entered in such a respectful manner, he believed, the land would open to him.

Barry Lopez
"The Country of the Mind,"
Arctic Dreams

The spiritual path is not like the interstate, with friendly green signs to tell us which exit is which and how to get to Los Angeles or Houston. It is much more like being dropped into the wilderness. We have to figure out which way to go by moving along, by being curious, by experimenting. Most of all, we need to trust our instincts and our innate sense of direction.

To follow the path, or the Tao, in the ancient Buddhist or Taoist sense, is to explore the terrain of our mind and feelings and to remain open to what we see and hear. The Path is not just something we follow, it is something we create as we go. How we make our way through the woods may not be the same as someone else's way. When our friend goes north, we may go south. In this sense, intention functions as our compass. It gives us direction and consistency and allows us to ask ourselves: "Am I following my intention or have I lost it somewhere along the way?"

Lewis Richmond
Work as a Spiritual Practice

"The Trail Is Not a Trail"

I drove down the Freeway
And turned off at an exit
And went along a highway
Til it came to a sideroad
Drove up the sideroad
Til it turned to a dirt road
Full of bumps, and stopped.
Walked up a trail
But the trail got rough
And it faded away—
Out in the open,
Every where to go.

Gary Snyder
*Left Out in the Rain:
New Poems 1947–1985*

Since Copernicus we have known better than to see the earth as the center of the universe. Since Einstein, we have learned that there is no center; or alternatively, that any point is as good as any other for observing the world. I take this to be roughly what medieval theologians meant when they defined God as a circle whose circumference is nowhere and whose center is everywhere. I find a kindred lesson in the words of the Zen master, Thich Nhat Hanh: "This spot where you sit is your own spot. It is on this very spot and in this very moment that you can become enlightened. You don't have to sit beneath a special tree in a distant land." There are no privileged locations. If you stay put, your place may become a holy center, not because it gives you special access to the divine, but because in your stillness you hear what might be heard anywhere. All there is to see can be seen from anywhere in the universe, if you know how to look; and the influence of the entire universe converges on every spot.

Scott Russell Sanders
"Settling Down,"
*Staying Put: Making a
Home in a Restless World*

A sacred site could be a cave, a rock, a pool, anywhere where a big snake could be or where he comes now and then. I'm not talking about a real snake in the sense of something you can see, I'm talking about a very old spiritual thing. I suppose a white person's sacred site might be his church, but you know when that church was built and you can feel it with your hands. Our sacred sites are more to do with the spirits, and they can't be dated because they've always been there.

Jack McPhee
Aboriginal Australian elder

"My Help Is in the Mountain"

My help is in the mountain
Where I take myself to heal
The earthly wounds
That people give to me.
I find a rock with sun on it
And a stream where the water runs gentle
And the trees which one by one give me company.
So must I stay for a long time
Until I have grown from the rock
And the stream is running through me
And I cannot tell myself from one tall tree.
Then I know that nothing touches me
Nor makes me run away.
My help is in the mountain
That I take away with me.

Nancy Wood
Hollering Sun

. . . What I want to speak for is not so much the
wilderness uses, valuable as those are, but the wilderness idea, which is a resource in itself. Being an intangible and spiritual resource, it will seem mystical to the
practical-minded—but then anything that cannot be
moved by a bulldozer is likely to seem mystical to
them.

I want to speak for the wilderness idea as something
that has helped form our character and that has certainly shaped our history as a people. It has no more
to do with recreation than churches have to do with
recreation, or than the strenuousness and optimism and
expansiveness of what historians call the "American
Dream" have to do with recreation. Nevertheless, since
it is only in this recreation survey that the values of
wilderness are being compiled, I hope you will permit
me to insert this idea between the leaves, as it were, of
the recreation report.

Something will have gone out of us as a people if
we ever let the remaining wilderness be destroyed;
if we permit the last virgin forests to be turned into
comic books and plastic cigarette cases; if we drive the
few remaining members of the wild species into zoos
or to extinction; if we pollute the last clear air and
dirty the last clean streams and push our paved roads
through the last of the silence, so that never again will
Americans be free in their own country from the noise,
the exhausts, the stinks of human and automotive
waste. And so that never again can we have the chance

to see ourselves single, separate, vertical and individual in the world, part of the environment of trees and rocks and soil, brother to the other animals, part of the natural world and competent to belong in it. Without any remaining wilderness we are committed wholly, without chance for even momentary reflection and rest, to a headlong drive into our technological termite-life, the Brave New World of a completely man-controlled environment. We need wilderness preserved—as much of it as is still left, and as many kinds—because it was the challenge against which our character as a people was formed. The reminder and the reassurance that it is still there is good for our spiritual health even if we never once in ten years set foot in it. It is good for us when we are young, because of the incomparable sanity it can bring briefly, as vacation and rest, into our insane lives. It is important to us when we are old simply because it is there—important, that is, simply as an idea.

Wallace Stegner
"Coda: Wilderness Letter," written for a 1960
recreation report and reprinted in
The Sound of Mountain Water

We need the tonic of wildness. . . . At the same time that we are earnest to explore and learn all things, we require that all things be mysterious and unexplorable, that land and sea be infinitely wild, unsurveyed, and unfathomed by us because unfathomable. We can never have enough of nature. We must be refreshed by the sight of inexhaustible vigor, vast and titanic features. . . .

Henry David Thoreau
Walden

When the questions are too big,
and the answers are not yet in time,
I look to the sky.

In starlight there are answers
to newer, older unframed questions.

Ancient light, our reassurance,
emitted with or without hope,
to be caught by a loving, skyward eye.

F. Lynne Bachleda

Over our striving, our rooms, our houses the beautiful
ritual of the rain falling against the window, the voice
of the wind, makes us remember a journey older than
thought, deeper than death, a triumph, the secret
ascension of love. The tasting of these things in our
days and nights is the partaking of the sacrament of
existence.

Cecil Collins
The Vision of the Fool

———

"Sacrament"

God, I have sought you as a fox seeks chickens,
curbing my hunger with cunning.
The times I have tasted your flesh
there was no bread and wine between us,
only night and the wind beating the grass.

Alden Nowlan
An Exchange of Gifts

. . . we need to go to the earth, as the source whence we came, and ask for its guidance, for the earth carries the psychic structure as well as the physical form of every living being upon the planet. Our confusion is not only within ourselves; it concerns also our role in the planetary community. Even beyond the earth, we need to go to the universe and inquire concerning the basic issues of reality and value, for, even more than the earth, the universe carries the deep mysteries of our existence within itself.

We cannot discover ourselves without first discovering the universe, the earth, and the imperatives of our own being. Each of these has a creative power and a vision far beyond any rational thought or cultural creation of which we are capable.

Thomas Berry
"The Dream of the Earth:
Our Way into the Future,"
The Dream of the Earth

TWO

TO MARVELING AND ADORATION

What arises as we observe our natural surroundings

Marveling and adoration are inevitable. Preoccupied though we may be, once outside it's natural to begin reading nature's bill-boards, like the blazing, beating, stifling, shivering, drenching, or balmy weather, for example. The fine print of the frog's eye will finally come into view if we allow enough time to permit the more wily motifs of subtle and shiny brilliance to penetrate.

Some years ago, when I had taken a job directing a writing program in St. Louis, Missouri, I often used color as a tonic. Regardless of the oasis-eyed student in my office, or the last itchlike whim of the secretary, or the fumings of the hysterically anxious chairman, I tried to arrive home at around the same time every evening, to watch the sunset from the large picture window in my living room, which overlooked Forest Park. Each night the sunset surged with purple pampas-grass plumes, and shot fuchsia rockets into the pink sky, then deepened through folded layers of peacock green to all the blues of India and a black across which clouds sometimes churned like alabaster dolls. The visual opium of the sunset was what I craved. Once, while eating a shrimp-and-avocado salad at the self-consciously stately faculty club, I found myself restless for the day to be over and all such tomblike encounters to pale, so I could drag my dinette-set chair up to the window and purge my senses with the pure color and visual tumult of the sunset. This happened again the next day in the coffee room, where I stood chatting with one of the literary historians, who always wore the drabbest camouflage colors and continued talking long after a point had been made. I set my facial muscles at "listening raptly," as she chuntered on about her specialty, the Caroline poets, but in my mind the sun was just beginning to set, a green glow was giving way to streaks of sulfur yellow, and a purple cloud train had begun staggering across the horizon. I was paying too much rent for my apartment, she explained. True, the apartment overlooked the park's changing seasons, had a picture window that captured the sunset every night, and was only a block away from a charming cobblestone area full of art galleries, antique stores, and ethnic restaurants. But this was all an *expense,* as she put it, with heavy emphasis on the second syllable, not just financial expense, but a too-extravagant experience of life. That evening, as I watched the sunset's pinwheels of apricot and mauve slowly explode into red ribbons, I thought: *The sensory misers will inherit the earth, but first they will make it not worth living on.*

When you consider something like death, after which (there being no news flash to the contrary) we may well go out like a candle flame, then it probably doesn't matter if we try too hard, are awkward sometimes, care for one another too deeply, are excessively curious about nature, are too open to experience, enjoy a nonstop expense of the senses in an effort to know life intimately and lovingly. It probably doesn't matter if, while trying to be modest and eager watchers of life's many spectacles, we sometimes look clumsy or get dirty or ask stupid questions or reveal our ignorance or say the wrong thing or light up with wonder like the children we all are. It probably doesn't matter if a passerby sees us dipping a finger into the moist pouches of dozens of lady's slippers to find out what bugs tend to fall into them, and thinks us a bit eccentric. Or a neighbor, fetching her mail, sees us standing in the cold with our own letters in one hand and a seismically red autumn leaf in the other, its color hitting our senses like a blow from a stun gun, as we stand with a huge grin, too paralyzed by the intricately veined gaudiness of the leaf to move.

Diane Ackerman
"Color,"
A Natural History of the Senses

They were letting off fireworks down at the waterfront,
the sky exploding in grenades of color. Whatever it is
that pulls the pin, that hurls you past the boundaries of
your own life into a brief and total beauty, even for a
moment, it is enough.

Jeannette Winterson
Gut Symmetries

The air still seems to reverberate with the wooden
sound of numskulls being soundly hit.

Edith Sitwell

Earth's crammed with heaven,
And every common bush afire with God;
But only he who sees, takes off his shoes—
The rest sit round it and pluck blackberries.

Elizabeth Barrett Browning
"Aurora Leigh," *Book VII*

And the voice of God comes to us,
as it came to Moses long ago by a burning bush:
"Take off your shoes;
the earth on which you stand is holy ground,
for I have hallowed it with my care and compassion
    since time began."

Forgive us, O God, when we have eyes and do not see
    the beauty of your creation;
Forgive us, O God, when we have ears and do not hear
    the wondrous music of heavenly spheres,
not to mention the birds beneath our own windows.
Forgive us our poverty of the senses;
and the shallowness of our sense of awe;
and our misunderstanding of value as we put dollar
    signs on your other species,
even as we destroy them.

Your whole universe, O God, O Creator, is a burning
    bush.
It calls us to turn aside, to pay attention,
to see and hear and sense—and to wonder and to praise,
Grant us new eyes, new ears, and newly awakened
    hearts;
to enter into your courts of nature
    and praise your holy presence here.

Elizabeth Dodson Gray

"I Got the Sun in the Morning"

Taking stock of what I have and what I haven't,
What do I find?
The things I've got will keep me satisfied.
Checking up on what I have and what I haven't.
What do I find?
A healthy balance on the credit side.

Got no diamond, got no pearl, still I think I'm a lucky
    girl,
I got the sun in the morning and the moon at night.
Got no mansion, got no yacht, still I'm happy with
    what I've got.
I got the sun in the morning and the moon at night.

Sunshine gives me a lovely day.
Moonlight gives me the Milky Way.

Got no checkbooks, got no banks, still I'd like to
    express my thanks.
I got the sun in the morning and the moon at night.
And with the sun in the morning and the moon in the
    evening, I'm all right.

Irving Berlin

Once or twice I have been asked what the peacock is "good for"—a question which gets no answer from me because it deserves none.

Flannery O'Connor
"The King of Birds,"
Mystery and Manners

———

There was a time when meadow, grove, and stream,
The earth, and every common sight,
To me did seem
Apparelled in celestial light,
The glory and freshness of a dream.

William Wordsworth
"Ode, Intimations of Immortality"
Stanza I

At last I was nearing the Big Rocks, a pair of enormous glacial erratics situated near the northwest corner of the pond. Normally the lower of the two boulders sits several feet in the water, but now both lay completely beached. I approached them with a growing anticipation mixed with apprehension. I could not conceive what profound cries or utterances such towering forms might make, and was ready to cover my ears, if necessary.

But unexpectedly, they did not speak at all. Rather, they *sang*—softly, with all the reserve of their great masses and strength: a high, falsetto song, arched and drawn out, such as great whales make, unheard by us, beneath their sea. It seemed not only to contain all previous sounds made by the rocks and fallen trees, but to carry the cry of all creation, deteriorating like a cherished face in the rain of time.

Their enormous, ice-rounded bulks moved through the night like the measures of their song. I followed them as far as I dared, and it seemed that if a wind had come up then, I might have been swept away for good.

I think it is only at times of such extraordinary outer calm, and inner fullness, that we hear such voices in nature.

Robert Finch
Outlands

No matter how sophisticated you may be, a large
granite mountain cannot be denied—it speaks in
silence to the very core of your being. There are some
that care not to listen but the disciples are drawn to the
high altar with magnetic certainty, knowing that a
great Presence hovers over the ranges.

Ansel Adams
Ansel Adams: An Autobiography

"To Earth, Mother of All"
Homeric Hymn XXX

I shall sing of well-formed Earth, mother of all
and oldest of all, who nourishes all things living on
    land.
Her beauty nurtures all creatures that walk upon the
    land,
and all that move in the deep or fly in the air.
O mighty one, you are the source of fair children and
    goodly fruit,
and on you it depends to give life to, or take it away
    from,
mortal men. Blessed is the man you favor
with willing heart, for he will have everything in
    abundance.

Homer
Translated by
Apostolos N. Athanassakis,
The Homeric Hymns

"The Bear"

In the huge, wide-open, sleeping eye of the mountain
The bear is the gleam in the pupil
Ready to awake
And instantly focus.

The bear is glueing
Beginning to end
With glue from people's bones
In his sleep.

The bear is digging
In his sleep
Throught the wall of the Universe
With a man's femur.
The bear is a well

Too deep to glitter
Where your shout
Is being digested.
The bear is a river

Where people bending to drink
See their dead selves.

The bear sleeps
In a kingdom of walls
In a web of rivers.

He is the ferryman
To dead land.

His price is everything.

Ted Hughes

... To encounter a truly wild animal on its own ground is to know the defeat of thought, to feel reason overpowered.

Barry Lopez
"The Passing Wisdom of Birds,"
Crossing Open Ground

The green turtle could find its way from the coast of Brazil to tiny Ascension Island in the middle of the Atlantic, 1,2000 miles away, where they nested, said Archie Carr in his book *So Excellent a Fishe*, " . . . it really seems impossible that turtles or terns could ever gather at Ascension—and yet they do." Take into account the theory of celestial navigation as it might apply to turtles, or of inertial-sense dead reckoning, or piloting with landmarks unknown to us, or response to the Coriolis force, and then logically knock each of them out, as he did, and you were left with the irreducible fact that either all these factors were involved or that there was some sense in them that we knew nothing about. The great mystery in terns or turtles was their inner synchronization with the changing conditions and ranges of the planet. That may be why some of us, still circling, backtracking, confused by our own directives, might be envious of them.

John Hay
"Homing," *The Undiscovered Country*

At flood time, the vulnerable snakes emerge from rocky ground and move upward, to hills and mounds, seeking refuge from the torrential waters that invade their homes. Silver with water, they wind about one another, slide over stones and through mud, and then rise up the rough trunks of trees where they wrap themselves around branches and wait out the storm. Gold-eyed, they stretch across the limbs, some looping down, some curled tight and nestlike between branch and trunk, their double tongues darting out like weather vanes. They remind me of women who know they are beautiful.

Linda Hogan
"Snake People,"
*Dwellings: A Spiritual History
of the Living World*

And your God is one God:
there is no God but The One,
the Compassionate,
the Merciful.

Behold, in the creation
of the heavens and the earth,
and the alternation of night and day,
and the ships that sail on the sea
to profit the people,
and the water God rains from the skies,
thereby enlivening the earth
after it has died,
and spreading animals of all kinds
thereupon,
and in the shifting of the winds
and the clouds
enslaved between the heavens and the earth:
therein are signs
for a discerning people.

The Prophet Muhammad
Translated by Thomas Cleary,
The Essential Koran

"Who Has Seen the Wind?"

Who has seen the wind?
Neither you nor I:
But when the trees bow down their heads,
The wind is passing by.

Christiana Rosetti

Earth . . . is a sparkling blue and white jewel . . . laced
with swirling veils of white . . . like a small pearl in a
thick sea of black mystery. . . . My view of our planet
was a glimpse of divinity.

Astronaut Edgar D. Mitchell
as quoted in *Earthspirit*

"To Know the Dark"

To know the dark with a light is to know the light.
To know the dark, go dark. Go without sight,
and find that the dark, too, blooms and sings,
and is traveled by dark feet and dark wings.

Wendell Berry
Selected Poems of Wendell Barry

The night became very dark. The rain surrounded the whole cabin with its enormous virginal myth, a whole world of meaning, of secrecy, of silence, of rumor. Think of it: all that speech pouring down, selling nothing, judging nobody, drenching the thick mulch of dead leaves, soaking the trees, filling the gullies and crannies of the wood with water, washing out the places where men have stripped the hillside! What a thing it is to sit absolutely alone, in the forest, at night, cherished by this wonderful, unintelligible, perfectly innocent speech, the most comforting speech in the world, the talk that rain makes by itself all over the ridges, and the talk of the water-courses everywhere in the hollows!

Nobody started it, nobody is going to stop it. It will talk as long as it wants, this rain. As long as it talks I am going to listen.

Thomas Merton
"Rain and the Rhinoceros,"
Raids on the Unspeakable

Form is certainty. All nature knows this, and we have no greater adviser. Clouds have forms, porous and shape-shifting, bumptious, fleecy. They are what clouds need to be, to be clouds. See a flock of them come, on the sled of the wind, all kneeling above the blue sea. And in the blue water, see the dolphin built to leap, the sea mouse skittering, see the ropy kelp with its air-filled bladders tugging it upward; see the albatross floating day after day on its three-jointed wings. Each form sets a tone, enables a destiny, strikes a note in the universe unlike any other. How can we ever stop looking? How can we ever turn away?

Mary Oliver
Blue Pastures

. . . The face of the water, in time, became a wonderful book—a book that was a dead language to the uneducated passenger, but which told its mind to me without reserve, delivering its most cherished secrets as clearly as if it uttered them with a voice. And it was not a book to be read once and thrown aside, for it had a new story to tell every day. Throughout the long twelve hundred miles there was never a page that was void of interest, never one that you could leave unread without loss, never one that you would want to skip, thinking you could find higher enjoyment in some other thing. There never was so wonderful a book written by man; never one whose interest was so absorbing, so unflagging, so sparklingly renewed with every re-perusal.

. . . I still keep in mind a certain wonderful sunset which I witnessed when steamboating was new to me. A broad expanse of the river was turned to blood; in the middle distance the red hue brightened into gold, through which a solitary log came floating, black and conspicuous; in one place a long, slanting mark lay sparkling upon the water; in another the surface was broken by boiling, tumbling rings, that were as many-tinted as an opal; where the ruddy flush was faintest was a smooth spot that was covered with graceful circles and radiating lines, ever so delicately traced; the shore on our left was densely wooded, and the sombre shadow that fell from this forest was broken in one place by a long, ruffled trail that shone like silver; and high above the forest wall a clean-stemmed dead tree waved a single leafy bough that glowed like a flame in the unobstructed splendor that was flowing from the sun. There were graceful curves, reflected images, woody heights, soft distances; and over the whole scene, far and near, the dissolving lights drifted steadily, enriching it, every passing moment, with new marvels of coloring.

I stood like one bewitched.

Mark Twain
Life on the Mississippi

Then one August night in the dry season, with the moon down and starlight etching the tops of the trees, everything changed with wrenching suddenness. A great storm came up from the west and moved quickly toward where I sat. It began as a flickering of light on the horizon and a faint roll of thunder. In the course of an hour the lightning grew like a menacing organism into flashes that spread across the sky and illuminated the thunderhead section by section. The sound expanded into focused claps to my left, front, and right. Now the rain came walking through the forest with a hiss made oddly soothing by its evenness of pitch. At this moment the clouds rose straight up and even seemed to tilt a little toward me, like a gigantic cliff about to topple over. The brilliance of the flashes was intimidating. Here, I knew, was the greatest havoc that inanimate nature can inflict in a short span of time: 10,000 volts dropping down an ionizing path at 500 miles an hour and a countersurge in excess of 30,000 amperes back up the path at ten times that speed, then additional back-and-forth surges faster than the eye can follow, all perceived as a single flash and crack of sound. . . .

Edward O. Wilson
"Storm Over the Amazon,"
Antaeus

The mind I love must have wild places, a tangled orchard where dark damsons drop in heavy grass, an overgrown little wood, the chance of a snake or two, a pool that nobody's fathomed the depth of, and paths threaded with flowers planted by the mind.

Katherine Mansfield

When you take a flower in your hand and really look at it, it's your world for the moment. I want to give that world to someone else. I want them to see it whether they want to or not.

Georgia O'Keeffe

A child said, What is grass? fetching it to me with full
   hands,
How could I answer the child? I do not know what it is
   anymore than he.
I guess it must be the flag of my disposition, out of the
   hopeful green stuff woven.
Or I guess it is the handkerchief of the Lord,
A scented gift and remembrancer designedly dropt,
Bearing the owner's name someway in the corners, that
   we may see and remark, and say Whose?

Walt Whitman
"Song of Myself,"
Leaves of Grass

Of all the wonders of nature a tree in summer is
perhaps the most remarkable; with the possible excep-
tion of a moose singing "Embraceable You" in spats.

Woody Allen

Hope and the future for me are not in lawns and cultivated fields, not in towns and cities, but in the impervious and quaking swamps. When, formerly, I have analyzed my partiality for some farm which I had contemplated purchasing, I have frequently found that I was attracted solely by a few square rods of impermeable and unfathomable bog—a natural sink in one corner of it. That was the jewel which dazzled me. . . .

Yes, though you may think me perverse, if it were proposed to me to dwell in the neighborhood of the most beautiful garden that ever human art contrived, or else of a Dismal Swamp, I should certainly decide for the swamp. How vain, then, have been all your labors, citizens, for me!

My spirits infallibly rise in proportion to the outward dreariness.

Henry David Thoreau
"Walking"

To go into solitude, a man needs to retire as much from his chamber as from society. I am not solitary whilst I read and write, though nobody is with me. But if a man would be alone, let him look at the stars. The rays that come from those heavenly worlds will separate between him and what he touches. One might think the atmosphere was made transparent with this design, to give man, in the heavenly bodies, the perpetual presence of the sublime. Seen in the streets of cities, how great they are! If the stars should appear one night in a thousand years, how would men believe and adore; and preserve for many generations the remembrance of the city of God which had been shown! But every night come out these envoys of beauty, and light the universe with the admonishing smile.

Ralph Waldo Emerson
Nature

God, when you thought of a pine tree,
How did you think of a star?

Angela Morgan
"God the Artist," Stanza 1

He moves the mountains without their knowledge;
he overturns them in his rage.
He makes the earth tremble;
he shakes its pillars.
He commands the sun, and it does not shine;
he seals off the light of the stars.
He alone stretches out the skies
and treads on the waves of the seas.
He made the Bear and Orion,
the Pleiades and every constellation.
His wonders are past all reckoning,
his miracles beyond all counting.

Job 9:5–10

THREE

TO COMPREHENSION
AND JOY

The reverberations of observing the earthly countenance of God

Comprehension and joy are earthy neighbors. Life's conveyor belt moves us past such witnessed privacies as sea turtles laboring over their eggs. Miraculously, years and thousands of nests later, we are borne to sighting a last hatchling scrambling home to the unforgiving sea. Here is an ancient wellspring of understanding without words and delight without limits. Like the modest, trumpeting crocus in spring, the resting parade must dance the jig of joy. Play on. Play on.

Don't look for formulas—mystic or obscure. I give you
pure joy. Behold my works as that which you see.

Constantine Brancusi
Catalog to his 1933
New York exhibition

People from a planet without flowers would think we
must be mad with joy the whole time to have such
things about us.

Iris Murdoch

Forget not that the earth delights to feel your bare feet
and the winds long to play with your hair.

Kahlil Gibran

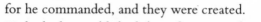

Praise ye the Lord.

Praise ye the Lord from the heavens: praise him in the heights.

Praise ye him and all his angels: praise ye him, all his hosts.

Praise ye him sun and moon: praise him, all ye stars of light.

Praise him, ye heavens of heavens, and ye waters that be above the heavens.

Let them praise the name of the Lord:

for he commanded, and they were created.

He hath also established them for ever and ever:

he hath made a decree which shall not pass.

Praise the Lord from the earth, ye dragons and all deeps:

Fire, and hail; snow and vapours; stormy wind fulfilling his word:

Mountains and all hills; fruitful trees and all cedars:

Beasts and all cattle; creeping things and flying fowl:

Kings of the earth, and all people, princes, and all judges of the earth:

Both young men, and maidens; old men, and children:

Let them praise the name of the Lord: for his name alone is excellent;

his glory is above the earth and heaven.

King David
Psalm 148:1–13

And I have loved thee, Ocean! and my joy
Of youthful sports was on thy breast to be
Borne, like thy bubbles, onward: from a boy
I wantoned with thy breakers, they to me
Were a delight; and if the freshening sea
Made them a terror, 'twas a pleasing fear,
For I was, as it were, a child of thee,
And trusted to thy billows far and near,
And laid my hand upon thy mane as I do here.

> George Gordon, Lord Byron
> "Canto IV," Stanza 184
> *Childe Harold's Pilgrimage*

If among the objects of the world of the spirit there is
something fixed and unalterable, great and illimitable,
something from which the beams of revelation, the
streams of knowledge, pour into the mind like water
into a valley, it is to be symbolized by a *mountain*.

> Islamic mystic Al-Ghazzali,
> ca. 1200 A.D.

So, if you cannot understand that there is something in man which responds to the challenge of this mountain and goes out to meet it, that the struggle is the struggle of life itself upward and forever upward, then you won't see why we go. What we get from this adventure is just sheer joy. And joy is, after all, the end of life. We do not live to eat and make money. We eat and make money to enjoy life. That is what life means and what life is for.

Sir George Mallory

Under the volcanoes, beside the snow-capped mountains, among the huge lakes, the fragrant, the silent, the tangled Chilean forest. . . . I have come out of that landscape, that mud, that silence, to roam, to go singing through the world.

Pablo Neruda

Inebriate of Air—am I—
And Debauchee of Dew—
Reeling through the endless summer days—
From inns of Molten Blue.

Emily Dickinson
No. 214, Stanza 2
The Poems of Emily Dickinson

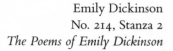

The great sea
Has sent me adrift.
It moves me
As the weed in a great river.
Earth and the great weather
Move me
Have carried me away
And move my inward parts with joy.

             Uvavnuk, Iglulik Eskimo

A bird does not sing because it has an answer. It sings
because it has a song.

             Chinese proverb

Let men their songs employ;
While fields and floods, rocks, hills and plains—
Repeat the sounding joy,
Repeat the sounding joy,
Repeat, repeat the sounding joy.

             Isaac Watts
         from Psalm 98 by King David

"Leave Krete And Come To This Holy Temple"

Leave Krete and come to this holy temple
where the graceful grove of apple trees
circles an altar smoking with frankincense.

Here roses leave shadows on the ground
and cold springs babble through apple branches
where shuddering leaves pour down profound sleep.

In our meadows where horses graze
and wild flowers of spring blossom,
anise shoots fill the air with aroma.

And here, Aphrodite, pour
heavenly nectar into gold cups
and fill them gracefully with sudden joy.

Sappho
Translated by Willis Barnstone

I know what it means to be a miner and a cowboy, and
have risked my life when need be, *but,* best of all, I
have felt the charm of the glorious freedom, the quick
rushing blood, the bounding motion, of the wild life,
the joy of the living and of the doing, of the mountain
and the plain; I have learned to know and feel some, at
least, of the secrets of the Wild Ones.

Grace Thompson–Seton
A Woman Tenderfoot

"Come Into Animal Presence"

Come into animal presence.
No man is so guileless as
the serpent. The lonely white rabbit
on the roof is a star
twitching its ears at the rain.
The llama intricately
folding its hind legs to be seated
not disdains but mildly
disregards human approval.
What joy when the insouciant
armadillo glances at us and doesn't
quicken his trotting
across the track into the palm bush.

What is this joy? That no animal
falters, but knows what it must do?
That the snake has no blemish,
that the rabbit inspects his strange surroundings
in white star-silence? The llama
rests in dignity, the armadillo
has some intention to pursue in the palm forest.
Those who were sacred have remained so,
holiness does not dissolve, it is a presence
of bronze, only the sight that saw it
faltered and turned from it.
An old joy returns in holy presence.

                                        Denise Levertov

I sat alone before my campfire one evening, watching as the sunset colors deepened to purple, the sky slowly darkened, and the stars came out. A deep peace lay over the woods and waters.

Gradually the wilderness around me merged into the blue of night. There was no sound save the crackle of my fire as the flames blazed around the birch and cedar logs.

The moon came up behind the black trees to the east, and the wilderness stood forth, vast, mysterious, still. All at once the silence and the solitude were touched by wild music, thin as air, the faraway gabbling of geese flying at night.

Presently I caught sight of them as they streamed across the face of the moon, the high, excited clamor of their voices tingling through the night, and suddenly I saw, in one of those rare moments of insight, what it means to be wild and free. As they went over me, I was there with them, passing over the moonlit countryside, glorying with them in their strong-hearted journeying, exulting in its joy and splendor.

The haunting voices grew fainter and faded in distance, but I sat on, stirred by a memory of something beautiful and ancient and now lost—a forgotten freedom we must all once have shared with other wild things, which only they and the wilderness can still recall to us, so that life becomes again, for a time, the wonderful, sometimes frightening, but fiercely joyous adventure it was intended to be.

Martha Reben
"Night Song," *A Sharing of Joy*

Seated here in solitude I have been musing over my life
—connecting events, dates, as links of a chain, neither
sadly nor cheerily, but somehow, today here under the
oak, in the rain, in an unusually matter-of-fact spirit.
But my great oak—sturdy, vital, green—five feet thick
at the butt; I sit a great deal near or under him. Then
the tulip tree near by—the Apollo of the woods—tall
and graceful, yet robust and sinewy, inimitable in hang
of foliage and throwing-out of limb, as if the beau-
teous, vital, leafy creature could walk, if it only would.
(I had a sort of dream-trance the other day, in which
I saw my favorite trees step out and promenade up,
down and around, very curiously—with a whisper
from one, leaning down as he passed me, "We do all
this on the present occasion exceptionally, just for
you.")

Walt Whitman
Specimen Days

. . . You New Yorkers will excuse me for missing my barred owls, ruffed grouse and snowshoe rabbits, my grosbeaks and deer. I love what you love too. In the city and in the country there is a simple, underlying basis to life which we forget almost daily: that life is good. We forget because losing it or wife, children, health, friends is so awfully painful, and because life is hard, but we know from our own experience as well as our expectations that it can and ought to be good, and is even *meant* to be good. Any careful study of living things, whether wolves, bears, or man, reminds one of the same direct truth; also of the clarity of the fact that evolution itself is obviously not some process of drowning beings clutching at straws and climbing from suffering and travail and virtual expiration to tenuous, momentary survival. Rather, evolution has been a matter of days well-lived, chameleon strength, energy, zappy sex, sunshine stored up, inventiveness, competitiveness, and the whole fun of busy brain cells. Watch how a rabbit loves to run; watch him set scenting puzzles for the terrier behind him. Or a wolf's amusement at the anatomy of a deer. Tug, tug, he pulls out the long intestines: ah, Yorick, how *long* you are! . . .

Edward Hoagland
"Thoughts on Returning to the City
after Five Months on a Mountain,"
Red Wolves and Black Bears

No; we have as usual been asking the wrong question. It does not matter a hoot what the mockingbird on the chimney is singing. . . . the real and proper question is: Why is it beautiful?

Annie Dillard
Pilgrim at Tinker Creek

"Dream Variation"

To fling my arms wide
In some place of the sun,
To whirl and to dance
Till the white day is done.
Then rest at cool evening
Beneath a tall tree
While night comes on gently,
  Dark like me—
That is my dream!

To fling my arms wide
In the face of the sun,
Dance! Whirl! Whirl!
Till the quick day is done.
Rest at pale evening . . .
A tall, slim tree . . .
Night coming tenderly
  Black like me.

Langston Hughes
Collected Poems

All my life through, the new sights of nature made me rejoice like a child.

Marie Curie

Pleasant walk yesterday, the most pleasant of days. At Walden Pond I found a new musical instrument which I call the ice-harp. A thin coat of ice covered a part of the pond, but melted around the edge of the shore. I threw a stone upon the ice which rebounded with a shrill sound, and falling again and again, repeated the note with pleasing modulation. I thought at first it was the "peep, peep" of a bird I had scared. I was so taken with the music that I threw down my stick and spent twenty minutes in throwing stones single or in handfuls on this crystal drum.

Ralph Waldo Emerson
The Journals of Ralph Waldo Emerson

In joy or sadness, flowers are our constant friends. We
eat, drink, sing, dance, and flirt with them. We wed
and christen with flowers. We dare not die without
them. We have worshipped with the lily, we have
meditated with the lotus, we have charged in battle
array with the rose and the chrysanthemum. We have
even attempted to speak in the language of flowers.
How could we live without them? It frightens one to
conceive of a world bereft of their presence. What
solace do they not bring to the bedside of the sick,
what a light of bliss to the darkness of weary spirits?
Their serene tenderness restores to us our waning
confidence in the universe even as the intent gaze of
a beautiful child recalls our lost hopes. When we are
laid low in the dust it is they who linger in sorrow
over our graves.

Kakuzo Okakura
The Book of Tea

Those who contemplate the beauty of the earth find
reserves of strength that will endure as long as life lasts.

Rachel Carson
The Sense of Wonder

I mention the spawning of the toads because it is one of the phenomena of spring which most deeply appeal to me, and because the toad, unlike the skylark and the primrose, has never had much of a boost from the poets. But I am aware that many people do not like reptiles or amphibians, and I am not suggesting that in order to enjoy the spring you have to take an interest in toads. There are also the crocus, the missel thrush, the cuckoo, the blackthorn, etc. The point is that the pleasures of spring are available to everybody and cost nothing. Even in the most sordid street the coming of spring will register itself by some sign or other, if it is only a brighter blue between the chimney pots or the vivid green of an elder sprouting on a blitzed site. Indeed it is remarkable how Nature goes on existing unofficially, as it were, in the very heart of London. . . .

At any rate, spring is here, even in London, N.1, and they can't stop you enjoying it. This is a satisfying reflection. How many a time have I stood watching the toads mating, or a pair of hares having a boxing match in the young corn, and thought of all the important persons who would stop me enjoying this if they could. But luckily they can't. So long as you are not actually ill, hungry, frightened or immured in a prison or a holiday camp, spring is still spring.

George Orwell
"Some Thoughts on the Common Toad,"
Shooting an Elephant and Other Essays

Go to the cicada, consider her ways and be wise. They stay long in the ground, but when they come out into the world, they sing at the top of their voice.

Sanki Ichikawa
"On the Japanese Cicada,"
Japan Quarterly

"I thank you god for most this amazing"

i thank You God for most this amazing
day:for the leaping greenly spirits of trees
and a blue true dream of sky;and for everything
which is natural which is infinite which is yes

(i who have died am alive again today,
and this is the sun's birthday;this is the birth
day of life and of love and wings:and of the gay
great happening illimitably earth)

how should tasting touching hearing seeing
breathing any—lifted from the no
of all nothing—human merely being
doubt unimaginable You?

(now the ears of my ears awake and
now the eyes of my eyes are opened)

E. E. Cummings

If I were to name the three most precious resources of life, I should say books, friends, and nature; and the greatest of these, at least the most constant and always at hand, is nature. Nature we have always with us, an inexhaustible storehouse of that which moves the heart, appeals to the mind, and fires the imagination—health to the body, a stimulus to the intellect, and joy to the soul. To the scientist Nature is a storehouse of facts, laws, processes; to the artist she is a storehouse of pictures; to the poet she is a storehouse of images, fancies, a source of inspiration; to the moralist, she is a storehouse of precepts and parables; to all she may be a source of knowledge and joy.

John Burroughs
"The Art of Seeing Things"

There came a sudden avalanche of tropical rain, crashing to earth, and immediately, in a small stream, small fish like sunfish leaped and whirled. A water snake, emerald-speckled on a throat distended by what must have been a still-live frog, swam clumsily away, disappearing into a black tunnel where the stream slipped into the jungle wall; at this moment, for the first time, the jungle came into focus for me. I could feel it, hear it, smell it all at once, could believe I was almost there.

Peter Matthiessen
The Cloud Forest

"Epirrhema"

Always in observing nature
Look at one and every creature;
Nothing's outside that's not within,
For nature has no heart or skin.
All at once that way you'll see
The sacred open mystery.

True seeming is the joy it gives,
The joy of serious playing;
No thing is single, if it lives,
But multiple its being.

Johann Wolfgang von Goethe
Translated by Michael Hamburger

A drowsy, half-wakeful menace waits for us in the quietness of this world. I have felt it near me while kneeling in the snow, minding a trap on a ridge many miles from home. There, in the cold that gripped my face, in the low, blue light failing around me, and the short day ending, in those familiar and friendly shadows, I was suddenly aware of something that did not care if I lived. Or, as it may be, running the river ice in mid-winter: under the sled runners a sudden cracking and buckling that scared the dogs and sent my heart racing. How swiftly the solid bottom of one's life can go.

John Haines
The Snow, the Stars, the Fire

A sea beach is a bad place to start thinking, but then so is almost anyplace. Anyplace where there's a leaf and an animal under it—an animal with someplace to go. Because where *is* it going—the seed hooked into your coat, and you yourself brother, where are *you* bound for? You think you know? In this house? On that street? You think you've arrived? You think you've lost your fur and your tail for a purpose spelled with a capital P and sold to you in some book that explains how everything was just a prelude until you came? If you do, you're happy I take it, and you'd be better off not to be following me or this crab or lifting up stones and looking under them.

For what you see under a stone may be like a flash of lightning before a traveler on a stormy night. It lights in one blue, glistening instant a hundred miles of devil's landscape such as he will never see again. Each stone, each tree, each ravine and crevice echoing and re-echoing with thunder will tell him, more than any daytime vision, of the road he travels. The flash hangs like an immortal magnification in the brain, and suddenly he knows the kind of country he passes over and the powers abroad in it. It is so in the country of Time; the flash lights a long way backward over a wild land.

Loren Eiseley
The Lost Notebooks of Loren Eiseley

I had a farm in Africa, at the foot of the Ngong Hills.
. . . The chief feature of the landscape, and of your
life in it, was the air. Looking back on a sojourn in
the African highlands, you are struck by your feeling
of having lived for a time up in the air. The sky was
rarely more than pale blue or violet, with a profusion
of mighty, weightless, ever-changing clouds towering
up and sailing on it, but it has a blue vigour in it, and
at a short distance it painted the ranges of hills and the
woods a fresh deep blue. In the middle of the day the
air was alive over the land, like a flame burning; it
scintillated, waved and shone like running water,
mirrored and doubled all objects, and created great
Fata Morgana. Up in this high air you breathed easily,
drawing in a vital assurance and lightness of heart. In
the highlands you woke up in the morning and
thought: Here I am, where I ought to be.

Isak Dinesen
"The Ngong Farm,"
Out of Africa

For my own part I am pleased enough with surfaces—in fact they alone seem to me to be of much importance. Such things for example as the grasp of a child's hand in your own, the flavor of an apple, the embrace of friend or lover, the silk of a girl's thigh, the sunlight on rock and leaves, the feel of music, the bark of a tree, the abrasion of granite and sand, the plunge of clear water into a pool, the face of the wind—what else is there? What else do we need?

Edward Abbey
"A Season in the Wilderness,"
Desert Solitaire

FOUR

TO CONNECTION AND UNITY

*What results from encountering the pieces of the whole
and the underlying order*

*Connection and unity are the elasticity in the web. Like Alice's
Wonderland, the world's possibilities stretch and shift, inviting
us in. Not strangers at the door, but ancient guests and hosts at
the round table, we can toast all the living. Food for all, and
all for food. The unification play is sublime, carnal, carnivorous,
vital, and lethal. The respiration of the Earth ties us to the
web, defines us within it. Audible and inaudible, a sigh, a cry,
or a whisper binds us together and blinds us to our supposed
differences.*

Jesus said, "I am he who exists from the undivided."
Jesus said, "It is I who am the light which is above
them all. It is I who am the all. From me did the all
come forth, and unto me did the all extend. Split a
piece of wood, and I am there. Lift up the stone, and
you will find me there."

Gospel of Thomas 61, 77

In everything you recognize yourself. The tiny beetle
that lies dead in your path—it was a living creature,
struggling for existence like yourself, rejoicing in the
sun like you, knowing fear and pain like you. And now
it is not more than decaying matter—which is what
you will be sooner or later too.

Albert Schweitzer
Reverence for Life: The Words of Albert Schweitzer

Many times I have looked into the eyes of wild animals
And we have parted friends.
What did they see, and recognize,
Shining through the windows of a human soul?

Grace Thompson-Seton
"Windows of the Soul," Stanza 9
The Singing Traveler

A weasel is wild. Who knows what he thinks? He sleeps in his underground den, his tail draped over his nose. Sometimes he lives in his den for two days without leaving. Outside, he stalks rabbits, mice, muskrats, and birds, killing more bodies than he can eat warm, and often dragging the carcasses home. Obedient to instinct, he bites his prey at the neck, either splitting the jugular vein at the throat or crunching the brain at the base of the skull, and he does not let go. One naturalist refused to kill a weasel who was socketed into his hand deeply as a rattlesnake. The man could in no way pry the tiny weasel off, and he had to walk half a mile to water, the weasel dangling from his palm, and soak him off like a stubborn label.

And once, says Ernest Thompson Seton, a man shot an eagle out of the sky. He examined the eagle and found the dry skull of a weasel fixed by the jaws to his throat. The supposition is that the eagle had pounced on the weasel and the weasel swiveled and bit as instinct taught him, tooth to neck, and nearly won. I would like to have seen that eagle from the air a few weeks or months before he was shot: was the whole weasel still attached to his feathered throat, a fur pendant? Or did the eagle eat what he could reach, gutting the living weasel with his talons before his breast, bending his beak, cleaning the beautiful airborne bones?

I have been reading about weasels because I saw one last week. I startled a weasel who startled me, and we exchanged a long glance.

Twenty minutes from my house, through the woods by the quarry and across the highway, is Hollins Pond, a remarkable piece of shallowness, where I like to go at sunset and sit on a tree trunk. . . .

The sun had just set. I was relaxed on the tree trunk, ensconced in the lap of lichen, watching the lily pads at my feet tremble and part dreamily over the thrusting path of a carp. A yellow bird appeared to my right and flew behind me. It caught my eye; I swiveled around—and next instant, inexplicably, I was looking down at a weasel, who was looking up at me.

Weasel! I'd never seen one wild before. He was ten inches long, thin as a curve, a muscled ribbon, brown as fruitwood, soft-furred, alert. His face was fierce, small and pointed as a lizard's; he would have made a good arrowhead. There was just a dot of chin, maybe two brown hairs' worth, and then the pure white fur began that spread down his underside. He had two black eyes I didn't see, any more than you see a window.

The weasel was stunned into stillness as he was emerging from beneath an enormous shaggy wild rose bush four feet away. I was stunned into stillness twisted backward on the tree trunk. Our eyes locked, and someone threw away the key.

Our look was as if two lovers, or deadly enemies, met unexpectedly on an overgrown path when each had been thinking of something else: a clearing blow to the gut. It was also a bright blow to the brain, or a sudden beating of brains, with all the charge and intimate grate of rubbed balloons. It emptied our lungs. It felled the forest, moved the fields, and drained the pond; the world dismantled and tumbled into that black hole of eyes. If you and I looked at each other that way, our skulls would split and drop to our shoulders. But we don't. We keep our skulls. So.

He disappeared. This was only last week, and already I don't remember what shattered the enchantment. I think I blinked, I think I retrieved my brain from the weasel's brain, and tried to memorize what I was seeing, and the weasel felt the yank of separation, the careening splashdown into real life and the urgent current of instinct. He vanished under the wild rose. I waited motionless, my mind suddenly full of data and my spirit with pleadings, but he didn't return.

Please do not tell me about "approach-avoidance conflicts." I tell you I've been in that weasel's brain for sixty seconds, and he was in mine. Brains are private places, muttering through unique and secret tapes—but the weasel and I both plugged into another tape simultaneously, for a sweet and shocking time. Can I help it if it was a blank?

What goes on in his brain the rest of the time? What does a weasel think about? He won't say. His journal is tracks in clay, a spray of feathers, mouse blood and bone: uncollected, unconnected, loose-leaf, and blown.

I would like to learn, or remember, how to live. I come to Hollins Pond not so much to learn how to live as, frankly, to forget about it. That is, I don't think I can learn from a wild animal how to live in particular—shall I suck warm blood, hold my tail high, walk with my footprints precisely over the prints of my hands?—but I might learn something of mindlessness, something of the purity of living in the physical senses and the dignity of living without bias or motive. The weasel lives in necessity and we live in choice, hating necessity and dying at the last ignobly in its talons. I would like to live as I should, as the weasel lives as he should. And I suspect that for me the way is like the weasel's: open to time and death painlessly, noticing everything, remembering nothing, choosing the given with a fierce and pointed will.

I missed my chance. I should have gone for the throat. I should have lunged for that streak of white under the weasel's chin and held on, held on through mud and into the wild rose, held on for a dearer life. We could live under the wild rose wild as weasels, mute and uncomprehending. I could very calmly go wild. I could live two days in the den, curled, leaning on mouse fur, sniffing bird bones, blinking, licking, breathing musk, my hair tangled in the roots of grasses. Down is a good place to go, where the mind is single. Down is out, out of your ever-loving mind and back to your careless senses. I remember muteness as a prolonged and giddy fast, where every moment is a feast of utterance received. Time and events are merely poured, unremarked, and ingested directly, like blood pulsed into my gut through a jugular vein. Could two live that way? Could two live under the wild rose, and explore by the pond, so that the smooth mind of each is as everywhere present to the other, and as received and as unchallenged, as falling snow?

We could, you know. We can live any way we want. People take vows of poverty, chastity, and obedience even of silence—by choice. The thing is to stalk your calling in a certain skilled and supple way, to locate the most tender and live spot and plug into that pulse. This is yielding, not fighting. A weasel doesn't "attack" anything; a weasel lives as he's meant to, yielding at every moment to the perfect freedom of single necessity.

I think it would be well, and proper, and obedient, and pure, to grasp your one necessity and not let it go, to dangle from it limp wherever it takes you. Then even death, where you're going no matter how you live, cannot you part. Seize it and let it seize you up aloft even, till your eyes burn out and drop; let your musky flesh fall off in shreds, and let your very bones unhinge and scatter, loosened over fields, over fields and woods, lightly, thoughtless, from any height at all, from as high as eagles.

Annie Dillard
"Living Like Weasels,"
Teaching a Stone to Talk

I think I could turn and live with animals, they are so placid and self-contain'd,
I stand and look at them long and long.

They do not sweat and whine about their condition,
They do not lie awake in the dark and weep for their sins,
They do not make me sick discussing their duty to God,
Not one is dissatisfied, not one is demented with the mania of owning things,
Not one kneels to another, nor to his kind that lived thousands of years ago,
Not one is respectable or unhappy over the whole earth.

Walt Whitman
Song of Myself

"Crows"

They give me a bad
reputation, those swart rowers
through the air, heavy winged
and heavy voiced, brass tipped.
Before us they lived here
in the tallest pine. Shortly
after coming I walked in
on a ceremony, the crows
were singing secretly
and beautifully a ritual.
They divebombed me. To make
peace I brought a sacrifice,
the remains of a leg
of lamb. Since then
we have had truce.
Smart, ancient, rowdy and far-
sighted, they use our land
as sanctuary for raiding
where men shoot at them.

They come down, settling
like unwieldy cargo jets, to the bird
food, scattering the
cardinals, the juncos. *God
they're big, I've never seen
them so near a house,*
the guest says. We look

at each other, the crows
and me. Outside
they allow my slow approach.
They do not touch our crops
even in the far garden
in the bottomland. I'm aware
women have been burned
for less. I stand
under the oldest white oak
whose arms coil fat as pythons
and scream at the hunters
driving them back
with black hair coarse and streaming:
Caw! Caw!

Marge Piercy
Circles on the Water

Standing on the bare ground, my head bathed by the blithe air, and uplifted into infinite space, all mean egotism vanishes. I become a transparent eye-ball; I am nothing; I see all; the currents of the Universal Being circulate through me; I am part or particle of God.

Ralph Waldo Emerson
Nature

I take a sun bath and listen to the hours, formulating, and disintegrating under the pines, and smell the resiny hardi-hood of the high noon hours. The world is lost in a blue haze of distances, and the immediate sleeps in a thin and finite sun.

Zelda Fitzgerald
Letter to F. Scott Fitzgerald

. . . God, I can push the grass apart
And lay my finger on Thy heart!

The world stands out on either side
No wider than the heart is wide;
Above the world is stretched the sky, —
No higher than the soul is high.
The heart can push the sea and land
Farther away on either hand;
The soul can split the sky in two,
And let the face of God shine through. . . .

Edna St. Vincent Millay
"Renascence"

On my travels in Tibet I was always delighted by the tradition of sky-burial. The human body is cut up and the bones broken to marrow and left for animals, mostly birds. Later the bones are pounded and mixed with tsampa—a roasted barley—and again offered to the animals. Finally everything is gone, gone back into the cycle. Recently, when a friend lost her beloved dog, she carried it out to a beautiful view of the mountains, covered it with wild flowers, and left it for the coyotes and ravens and bugs. We should have the courage to do the same for ourselves, to re-enter the great cycle of feeding.

Jack Turner
The Abstract Wild

———

I wonder if anyone else has an ear so tuned and sharpened as I have, to detect the music, not of the spheres, but of earth, subtleties of major and minor chord that the wind strikes upon the tree branches. Have you ever heard the earth breathe. . . ?

Kate Chopin

"Breaths"

Listen more often
To things than to beings;
The fire's voice is heard,
Hear the voice of water.
Hear in the wind
The bush sob:
It is the ancestors' breath.

Those who died have never left,
They are in the brightening shadow
And in the thickening shadow;
The dead are not under earth,
They are in the rustling tree,
They are in the groaning woods,
They are in the flowing water,
They are in the still water,
They are in the hut, they are in the crowd.
The dead are not dead.

They are in the rustling tree,
They are in the groaning woods,
They are in the flowing water,
They are in the still water,
They are in the hut, they are in the crowd.
The dead are not dead.

Birago Diop, a Senegalese writer

As I get older, I burrow more and more into the hills. The Great Spirit made them for us, for me. I want to blend with them, shrink into them, and finally disappear in them. . . . All of nature is in us, all of us is in nature. That is as it should be.

Pete Catches
Sioux medicine man

I said in mine heart concerning the estate of the sons
   of men,
that God might manifest them,
and that they might see that they themselves are beasts;
even one thing befalleth them:
as the one dieth, so dieth the other;
   yea, they all have one breath;
so that a man hath no preeminence over a beast;
for all is vanity.
All go unto one place;
all are of the dust, and all turn to dust again.

Solomon
Ecclesiastes 3:18–20

One perfect Nature pervades and
circulates within all natures.
One all-inclusive Reality contains
and embraces all realities.
One moon is reflected in every
expanse of water.
Every reflected moon
is the one moon.
The essence of all the Buddhas
is in my being.
My essence is in their being.
The Inner Light is beyond
good and bad.
Like space it knows no boundaries.
It is here right now, within us,
always full and serene.
Only when you hunt for it
do you miss it.
You can't grasp it, but
you can't lose it.
It winds its own way.
When you are silent, it speaks.
When you speak, it is dumb.
There are no obstacles.
The great gate of love is wide open.

Yung-Chia Ta-Shih
7th–8th century Chinese Zen Buddhist master

One you think should be hit is none else but you.

One you think should be governed is none else but you.

One who you think should be be tortured is none else but you.

One who you think should be enslaved is none else but you.

One who you think should be killed is none else but you.

A sage is ingenuous and leads his life after comprehending the parity of the killed and the killer.

Therefore, neither does he cause violence to others, nor does he make others do so.

Acaangasutra 5, 101–2
Jain sacred text

For thousands and thousands of years I existed as a rock. Then I died and became a plant. For thousands and thousands of years I existed as a plant. Then I died and became a fish. For thousands and thousands of years I existed as a fish. Then I died and became an animal. For thousands and thousands of years I existed as an animal. Then I died and became a human being. Tell me, what have I ever lost by dying?

Jellaladin Rumi
13th century Sufi mystic

I wandered lonely as a cloud
That floats on high o'er vales and hills,
When all at once I saw a crowd,
A host, of golden daffodils;
Beside the lake, beneath the trees,
Fluttering and dancing in the breeze.

> William Wordsworth
> "I Wandered Lonely as a Cloud"

The forest is one big thing; it has people, animals and plants. There is no point saving the animals if the forest is burned down; there is no point saving the forest if the people and animals who live in it are killed or driven away. The groups trying to save the animals cannot win if the people trying to save the forest lose. . . .

> Paiakan
> Amazon rain forest Kayapo tribe leader

[All] who have achieved real excellence in any art possess one thing in common, that is, a mind to obey nature, to be one with nature, throughout the four seasons of the year.

Matsuo Basho
Translated by Nobuyuki Yuasa
The Narrow Road to the Deep North
& Other Travel Sketches

Imagine a ruin so strange it must never have happened.

First, picture the forest. I want you to be its conscience, the eyes in the trees. The trees are columns of slick, brindled bark like muscular animals overgrown beyond all reason. Every space is filled with life: delicate, poisonous frogs war-painted like skeletons, clutched in copulation, secreting their precious eggs onto dripping leaves. Vines strangling their own kin in the everlasting wrestle for sunlight. The breathing of monkeys. A glide of snake belly on branch. A single-file army of ants biting a mammoth tree into uniform grains and hauling it down to the dark for their ravenous queen. And, in reply, a choir of seedlings arching their necks out of rotted tree stumps, sucking life out of death. This forest eats itself and lives forever.

Barbara Kingsolver
The Poisonwood Bible

Far from separating human beings from the rest of creation, Hinduism sees them as integral parts of an organic whole. All beings and things are the creation of the Supreme and therefore united and connected. The Sankrit phrase *Tat twam asi* is known by all Hindus: "Thou art that." It was therefore possible for the smiling Indian yogi to say to the British soldier who bayoneted him in the stomach: "I am thou."

The whole of nature is seen as vibrating with life: trees, rocks and waterfalls become shrines; mountains and forests symbolize the power of nature. While spiritually advanced yogis seek desolate regions or wildernesses in order to discover ultimate reality, the broad masses travel to rivers, which are seen as the source and support of spiritual life—the symbol of life without end.

Peter Marshall
Nature's Web: Rethinking Our Place on Earth

Now nearly all those I loved and did not understand when I was young are dead, but I still reach out to them.

Of course, now I am too old to be much of a fisherman and now of course I usually fish the big waters alone although some friends think I shouldn't. Like many fly fishermen in western Montana where the summer days are almost Arctic in length, I often do not start fishing until the cool of the evening. Then in the Arctic half-light of the canyon, all existence fades to a being with my soul and memories and the sounds of the Big Blackfoot River and a four-count rhythm and the hope that a fish will rise.

Eventually, all things merge into one, and a river runs through it. The river was cut by the world's great flood and runs over rocks from the basement of time. On some of the rocks are timeless raindrops. Under the rocks are the words, and some of the words are theirs. I am haunted by waters.

Norman Maclean
A River Runs Through It

Once in a lifetime, perhaps, one escapes the actual confines of the flesh. Once in a lifetime, if one is lucky, one so merges with sunlight and air and running water that whole eons, the eons that mountains and deserts know, might pass in a single afternoon without discomfort. The mind has sunk away into its beginnings among old roots and the obscure tricklings and movings that stir inanimate things. Like the charmed fairy circle into which a man once stepped, and upon emergence learned that the whole century had passed in a single night, one can never quite define this secret; but it has something to do, I am sure, with common water. Its substance reaches everywhere; it touches the past and prepares the future; it moves under the poles and wanders thinly in the heights of the air. It can assume forms of exquisite perfection in a snowflake, or strip the living to a single shining bone cast up by the sea.

Loren Eiseley
The Immense Journey

For the sea lies all about us . . . In its mysterious past it encompasses all the dim origins of life and receives in the end, after, it may be, many transmutations, the dead husks of that same life. For all at last return to the sea—to Oceanus, the ocean river, like the ever-flowing stream of time, the beginning and the end.

Rachel Carson
The Sea Around Us

A scientist will tell you that it's all connected—that if you live in Texas you must protect the honor and integrity of that country's core, for you are tied to it, it is as much a part of you as family—but if you are a child and given to daydreaming and wondering, I believe that you'll understand this by instinct. You don't need proof that the water moving through those shady creeks up in the wild hills and mountains is the same that later moves through your body. You can instead stand outside—even in the city, even in such a place as Houston, and look north with the wind in your face (or with a salt breeze at your back, carrying your essence back to the hill country like an offering), and you can feel the tremble and shimmer of that magic underground river, the yearning and timelessness of it, just beneath your seven-year-old feet. You can know of the allegiance you owe it, can sense this in a way that not even the scientists know. It is more like the way when you are in your mother's arms, or your grandmother's, that you know it's all tied together, and that someday you are going to understand it all.

Rick Bass
"On Willow Creek,"
Wild to the Heart

A black rat snake, like the good climber his breed is, had slithered up the side of the honey house and was looped around the nest calmly swallowing the two baby birds. I ran outside, grabbed the snake by the tail and shook him hard. The baby birds dropped from his mouth, wet but undigested. I threw the snake as far as I could, scooped up the babies and put them back in the nest. The parent birds remained in a state of ineffectual confusion all day, alternately repelled by and drawn to their offspring. At nightfall they finally returned, and the pair of young phoebes lived to fly from the nest on their own.

And there we are, with my meddling, back to the human responsible for putting a flock of chickens in prime mouse habitat, setting the process in motion in the first place. I like to think of it as a circle. If I take one step out of the center, I find myself a part of that circle—a circle made of chickens, chopped corn, mice, snakes, phoebes, me, and back to the chickens again, a tidy diagram that only hints at the complexity of the whole. For each of us is a part of other figures, too, the resulting interconnecting whole faceted, weblike, subtle, flexible, fragile. As a human being I am a great meddler; I fiddle, alter, modify. This is neither good nor bad, merely human, in the same way that the snake who eats mice and phoebes is merely serpentish. But being human I have the kind of mind which can recognize that when I fiddle and twitch any part of the circle there are reverberations throughout the whole.

Sue Hubbell
A Country Year:
Living the Questions

The man who sat on the ground in his tipi meditating on life and its meaning, accepting the kinship of all creatures and acknowledging unity with the universe of things was infusing into his being the true essence of civilization.

Luther Standing Bear
Ogala Sioux

Surrounded by the mountain walls, I drift off in daydreams, as if I've sunk into the island itself. Winds of an ancient dawn eddy over me. Dewdrops trickle across. my face and seep into my opened pores. Blood flows like lava through a maze of veins beneath my chilled and hardened skin. Moss grows over my cheeks, covers my hands and legs. Tendrils and rootlets probe the cooling crevices of my flesh. A spider drifts down on a thread of iridescent silk, crawls across the bareness of my belly, weaves a web in the corner of my eye. Voles burrow toward the bedrock of my bones. A deer's hooves press into my chest. Fish swim in the black pools of my eyes. Birds nest in my hair. Runnels of water flow over my thighs, pool in the crater between my ribs, spill across my cheeks. The sea crashes at my sides and wears them away. I become smaller and smaller, and vanish forever beneath the tide.

Richard Nelson
The Island Within

The world of life, of spontaneity, the world of dawn
and sunset and starlight, the world of soil and sunshine,
of meadow and woodland, of hickory and oak and
maple and hemlock and pineland forests, of wildlife
dwelling around us, of the river and its well-being—all
of this some of us are discovering for the first time as
the integral community in which we live. Here we
experience the reality and the values that evoke in us
our deepest moments of reflection, our revelatory
experience of the ultimate mystery of things. Here, in
this intimate presence to the valley in all its vitality, we
receive those larger intuitions that lead us to dance and
sing, intuitions that activate our imaginative powers in
their most creative functions. This, too, is what in-
spires our weddings, our home life, and our joy in our
children. Even our deepest human sensitivities emerge
from our region, our place, our specific habitat, for the
earth does not give itself to us in a global sameness. It
gives itself to us in arctic and tropical regions, in seashore
and desert, in prairielands and woodlands, in mountains and valleys. Out of each a unique shaping of life
takes place, a community, an integral community of all
the geological as well as the biological and the human
components. Each region is a single community so intimately related that any benefit or any injury is immediately experienced throughout the entire community.
So it is also with ourselves.

Thomas Berry
The Dream of Earth

Hopi Pueblo elders have said that the austere and, to some eyes, barren plains and hills surrounding their mesa-top villages actually help to nurture the spirituality of the Hopi way. The Hopi elders say that the Hopi people might have settled in locations far more lush where daily life was not so grueling. But there on the high silent sandstone mesas that overlook the sandy arid expanses stretching to all horizons, the Hopi elders say the Hopi people must "live by their prayers" if they are to survive. The Hopi way cherishes the intangible: the riches realized from interaction and interrelationships with all beings above all else. Great abundances of material things, even food, the Hopi elders believe, tend to lure human attention away from what is most valuable and important. . . .

The bare vastness of the Hopi landscape emphasizes the visual impact of every plant, every rock, every arroyo. Nothing is overlooked or taken for granted. Each ant, each lizard, each lark is imbued with great value simply because the creature is there, simply because the creature is alive in a place where any life at all is precious. Stand on the mesa edge at Walpai and look west over the bare distances toward the pale blue outlines of the San Francisco peaks where the ka'tsina spirits reside. So little lies between you and the sky. So little lies between you and the earth. One look and you know that simply to survive is a great triumph, that every possible resource is needed, every possible ally—even the most humble insect or reptile. You realize you will be speaking with all of them if you intend to last out the year. Thus it is that the Hopi elders are grateful to the landscape for aiding them in their quest as spiritual people.

Leslie Marmon Silko
"Interior and Exterior Landscapes,"
Yellow Woman and a Beauty of the Spirit

Harmony with creation is grounded deeply in one's relationship with the land. For most Native Americans, it is impossible to speak of a personal identity apart from the land. The earth grounds us not only geographically but psychologically. As my grandmother told me, when I lost touch with Mother Earth, I misbehaved. When I attended to the land, however, my behavior improved. In other words, the land itself can heal.

Michael Galvan
*Faith and Cultures:
A Multi-Cultural Catechetical Resource*

Sometimes I hear [the mysterious language of Earth] talking. The light of the sunflower was one language, but there are others more audible. Once, in the redwood forest, I heard a beat, something like a drum or heart coming from the ground and trees and wind. That underground current stirred a kind of knowing inside me, a kinship and longing, a dream barely remembered that disappeared back to the body. Another time, there was the booming voice of an ocean storm thundering from far out at sea, telling about what lived in the distance, about the rough water that would arrive, wave after wave revealing the disturbance at center.

Tonight I walk. I am watching the sky. I think of the people who came before me and how they knew the placement of stars in the sky, watched the moving sun long and hard enough to witness how a certain angle of light touched a stone only once a year. Without written records, they knew the gods of every night, the small, fine details of the world around them and of immensity above them. . . .

It's winter and there is smoke from the fires. The square, lighted windows of houses are fogging over. It is a world of elemental attention, of all things working together, listening to what speaks in the blood. Whichever road I follow, I walk in the land of many gods, and they love and eat one another. Walking, I am listening to a deeper way. Suddenly all my ancestors are behind me. Be still, they say. Watch and listen. You are the result of the love of thousands.

Linda Hogan
"Walking,"
*Dwellings: A Spiritual History
of the Living World*

FIVE

TO REDEMPTION AND GRACE

The peace of being held in place in the divine order

Redemption and grace surround us like mist—unbidden, unearned, quiet pearls of mysterious peace. These "old-fashioned" revival words will never lose their place when renewal of the soul is what's at stake. Newly assured of our place in the cosmic play, why not let mercy rain down, for whom has not known drought?

To rest, go to the woods
Where what is made is made
Without your thought or work.
Sit down; begin the wait
For small trees to grow big,
Feeding on earth and light.
Their good result is song
The winds must bring, the trees
Must wait to sing, and sing
Longer than you can wait.
Soon you must go. The trees,
Your seniors, standing thus
Acknowledged in your eyes,
Stand as your praise and prayer.
Your rest is in this praise
Of what you cannot be
And what you cannot do.

Wendell Berry
"The Farm," IX
A Timbered Choir:
The Sabbath Poems: 1979–1997

"Lost"

Stand still. The trees ahead and bushes beside you
Are not lost. Wherever you are is called Here,
And you must treat it as a powerful stranger,
Must ask permission to know it and be known.
The forest breathes. Listen. It answers,
I have made this place around you.
If you leave it, you may come back again, saying Here.
No two trees are the same to Raven
No two branches are the same to Wren.
If what a tree or a bush does is lost on you,
You are surely lost. Stand still. The forest knows
Where you are. You must let it find you.

David Wagoner

We all move on the fringes of eternity and are sometimes granted vistas through the fabric of illusion.

Ansel Adams
Ansel Adams: An Autobiography

Climb the mountains and get their good tidings.
Nature's peace will flow into you as sunshine flows
into trees. The winds will blow their own freshness
into you, and the storms their energy, while cares
drop off like autumn leaves.

John Muir

Man is a thinking reed but his great works are done
when he is not calculating and thinking. "Childlike-
ness" has to be restored with long years of training
in the art of self-forgetfulness. When this is attained,
man thinks yet he does not think. He thinks like the
showers coming down from the sky; he thinks like
the waves rolling on the ocean; he thinks like the stars
illuminating the nightly heavens; he thinks like the
green foliage shooting forth in the relaxing spring
breeze. Indeed, he is the showers, the ocean, the stars,
the foliage.

D.T. Suzuki
"Introduction,"
Zen in the Art of Archery

Anyway—why go into the desert? Really, why do it? That sun, roaring at you all day long. The fetid, tepid, vapid little water holes slowly evaporating under a scum of grease, full of cannibal beetles, spotted toads, horsehair worms, liver flukes, and down at the bottom, inevitably, the pale cadaver of a ten-inch centipede. Those pink rattlesnakes down in The Canyon, those diamondback monsters thick as a truck driver's wrist that lurk in shady places along the trail, those unpleasant solpugids and unnecessary Jerusalem crickets that scurry on dirty claws across your face at night. Why? The rain that comes down like lead shot and wrecks the trail, those sudden rockfalls of obscure origin that crash like thunder ten feet behind you in the heart of a dead-still afternoon. The ubiquitous buzzard, patient— but only so patient. . . .

On our second day there I walked down the stream, alone, to look at the canyon beyond. I entered the canyon and followed it for half the afternoon, for three or four miles maybe, until it became a gorge so deep, narrow and dark, full of water and the inevitable quagmires of quicksand, that I turned around and looked for a way out. A route other than the way I'd come, which was crooked and uncomfortable and buried— I wanted to see what was up on top of this world. I found a sort of chimney flue on the east wall, which looked plausible, and sweated and cursed my way up through that until I reached a point where I could walk upright, like a human being. Another 300 feet of scrambling brought me to the rim of the canyon. No one, I felt certain, had ever before departed Nasja Canyon by that route.

But someone had. Near the summit I found an arrow sign, three feet long, formed of stones and pointing off into the north toward those same old purple vistas, so grand, immense, and mysterious, of more canyons, more mesas and plateaus, more mountains, more cloud-dappled sunspangled leagues of desert sand and desert rock, under the same old wide and aching sky.

The arrow pointed into the north. But what was it pointing *at*? I looked at the sign closely and saw that those dark, desert-varnished stones had been in place for a long, long, time; they rested in compacted dust. They must have been there for a century at least. I followed the direction indicated and came promptly to the rim of another canyon and a drop-off straight down of a good 500 feet. Not that way, surely. Across this canyon was nothing of any unusual interest that I could see—only the familiar sun-blasted sandstone, a few scrubby clumps of blackbrush and prickly pear, a few acres of nothing where only a lizard could graze, surrounded by a few square miles of more nothingness interesting chiefly to horned toads. I returned to the arrow and checked again, this time with field glasses, looking away for as far as my aided eyes could see toward the north, for ten, twenty, forty miles into the distance. I studied the scene with care, looking for an ancient Indian ruin, a significant cairn, perhaps an abandoned mine, a hidden treasure of some inconceivable wealth, the mother of all mother lodes. . . .

But there was nothing out there. Nothing at all. Nothing but the desert. Nothing but the silent world. That's why.

Edward Abbey
Desert Solitaire: A Season in the Wilderness

The candle's wick topples and drowns. Perfect blackness releases me into the free and boundless night, to roam in dreams through an everlasting, untrammeled forest; a forest that gives me breath and shelters me; a spirit forest; a forest that envelops me with shining, consecrated webs and binds me here forever.

Richard Nelson
The Island Within

"The Lake Isle of Innisfree"

I will arise and go now, and go to Innisfree,
And a small cabin build there, of clay and wattles made:
Nine bean-rows will I have there, a hive for the
  honeybee,
And live alone in the bee-loud glade.

And I shall have some peace there, for peace comes
  dropping slow,
Dropping from the veils of the morning to where the
  cricket sings;
There midnight's all a glimmer, and noon a purple
  glow,
And evening full of the linnet's wings.

I will arise and go now, for always night and day
I hear lake water lapping with low sounds by the shore;
While I stand on the roadway, or on the pavements
  grey,
I hear it in the deep heart's core.

William Butler Yeats

I will lift up mine eyes unto the hills, from whence
    cometh my help.
My help cometh from the Lord, which made heaven
    and earth . . .
The Lord is thy keeper: the Lord is thy shade upon thy
    right hand.
The sun shall not smite thee by day, nor the moon by
    night.
The Lord shall preserve thee from all evil: he shall
    preserve thy soul.
The Lord shall preserve thy going out and thy coming
    in from this time forth,
and even for evermore.

King David
Psalm 121:1–2, 5–8

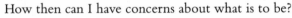

My Lord is boundless as the sun and moon,
Lighting heaven and earth;
How then can I have concerns about what is to be?

Man'Yoshu
Shinto poet

Don't be anxious about your life; what you'll have to eat and drink, or what you will wear to cover your body. Life is more than food, and the body is more than clothing. Look at the birds in the air. They don't sow or reap or harvest, and yet your Heavenly Father feeds them. Aren't you more valuable to him than the birds?

Who can add anything to his life span through being anxious? Why are you worried about clothing? Look at the lilies in the fields. They just grow, without needing to work or spin, yet even Solomon in all his glory was not so splendid. If God clothes the fields so magnificently, will he not clothe you? O men of little faith! Don't be anxious, saying, "What shall we eat?" or "What shall we wear?" Your Heavenly Father knows what you need. First seek his kingdom and his good- ness, and all these things shall be yours as well.

Gospel of Matthew 6:25–33

What need has nature of thought and care? In nature all things return to their common source and are dis- tributed along different paths through one action, the fruits of a hundred thoughts are realized. What need has nature of thought, of care?

Confucious
I Ching, Great Commentary 2.5.1

"Come Rain or Come Shine"

I'm gonna love you
Like nobody's loved you,
Come rain or come shine.
High as a mountain
And deep as a river,
Come rain or come shine.

I guess when you met me
It was just one of those things,
But don't ever bet me,
'Cause I'm gonna be true if you let me.

You're gonna love me
Like nobody's loved me
Come rain or come shine.
Happy together,
Unhappy together
And won't it be fine.

Days may be cloudy or sunny,
We're in or we're out of the money,
But I'm with you always,
I'm with you rain or shine!

Johnny Mercer

My heart in middle age found the Way,
And I came to dwell at the foot of this mountain.
When the spirit moves, I wander alone
Amid beauty that is all for me.

I will walk till the water checks my path,
Then sit and watch the rising clouds —
And some day meet an old wood-cutter
And talk and laugh and never return.

Wang Wei
7th century T'ang dynasty poet
Translated by Witter Bynner
The Jade Mountain

The universe was not made in jest but in solemn,
incomprehensible earnest. By a power that is unfath-
omably secret, and holy, and fleet. There is nothing
to be done about it, but ignore it, or see. And then
you walk fearlessly, eating what you must, growing
wherever you can. . . .

Annie Dillard
Pilgrim at Tinker Creek

No culture has yet solved the dilemma each has faced with the growth of the conscious mind: how to live a moral and compassionate existence when one is fully aware of the blood, the horror inherent in all life, when one finds darkness not only in one's own culture but within oneself. If there is a stage at which an individual life becomes truly adult, it must be when one grasps the irony in its unfolding and accepts responsibility for a life lived in the midst of such paradox. One must live in the middle of contradiction because if all contradiction were eliminated at once life would collapse. There are simply no answers to some of the great pressing questions. You continue to live them out, making your life a worthy expression of a leaning into the light.

Barry Lopez
Arctic Dreams

When the pain of leaving behind what we know outweighs the pain of embracing it, or when the power we face is overwhelming and neither fight nor flight will save us, there may be salvation in sitting still. And if salvation is impossible, then at least before perishing we may gain a clearer vision of where we are. By sitting still I do not mean the paralysis of dread, like that of a rabbit frozen beneath the dive of a hawk. I mean something like reverence, a respectful waiting, a deep attentiveness to forces much greater than our own.

Scott Russel Sanders
"Settling Down,"
Staying Put:
Making a Home in a Restless World

Where there is sunshine, there is also shade.

Kashmiri Proverb

I have a friend who feels sometimes that the world is hostile to human life—he says it chills us and kills us. But how could *we* be were it not for this planet that provided our very shape? Two conditions—gravity and a livable temperature range between freezing and boiling—have given us fluids and flesh. The trees we climb and the ground we walk on have given us five fingers and toes. The "place" (from the root *plat,* broad, spreading, flat) gave us far-seeing eyes, the streams and breezes gave us versatile tongues and whorly ears. The land gave us a stride, and the lake a dive. The amazement gave us our kind of mind. We should be thankful for that, and take nature's stricter lessons with some grace.

Gary Snyder
"The Place, The Region, The Commons,"
The Practice of the Wild

The winds of grace blow all the time. All we need to do is set our sails.

Ramakrishna

. . . We do not know on what errand they are bent, to
What mission committed. It is a world that
They live in, and it is their life.
They move through the world and breathe destiny.
Their destiny is as bright as crystal, as pure
As a dream of zero. Their destiny
Must resemble happiness even though they do not
    know that name. . . .

Robert Penn Warren
"Caribou,"
New and Selected Poems 1923–1985

I have listened by a thousand fires as the Buffalo Wind blew through our lives. . . . And so would come a flood of revelation, an unceasing flow of inspiration such as could not be courted. Many a time have I sat by the embers, in motionless silence for hours, while the words came in unhesitating rhythm of passionate life—for we did not measure our life together with a shallow cup. Each time we dipped, we brought up the chalice brimming full and running over.

Julia M. Seton
"Prologue,"
By a Thousand Fires

Nature is the great emptiness, the source, out of which our culture and all its flowering comes, and in order not to lose sight of this, not to become orphans lost in the minutiae of our daily lives, and, like the rich man's son starving outside his father's gate, to forget who we are, it is vital that wildness be preserved for its own sake, which is to say, for our sake.

Dan Gerber
"Walking in Tierra del Fuego,"
*Sacred Trusts: Essays on
Stewardship and Responsibility*

A wise elder among my people, the Tewa, frequently used the phrase *Pin pe obi,* "look to the mountaintop," while he was alive. I first heard it 25 years ago when I was seven years old, as I was practicing for the first time to participate in relay races we run in the Pueblo country to give strength to the sun father as he journeys across the sky. I was at one end of the earth track which ran east to west, like the path of the sun. The old man, who was blind, called me to him and said: "Young one, as you run look to the mountaintop," and he pointed to Tsikomo, the western sacred mountain of the Tewa world, which loomed off in the distance. "Keep your gaze fixed on that mountain, and you will feel the miles melt beneath your feet. Do this and in time you will feel as if you can leap over bushes, trees, and even the river. . . ."

I have come to understand that this old Tewa saw the whole of life as consisting of the dual quest for wisdom and for divinity, and he anchored his aspirations and his vision firmly onto that greatest, most immovable, and most enduring of the earth's natural monuments. He recognized clearly that to live is simply to seek knowledge and fulfillment on the one hand and redemption on the other. That is all.

Alphonso Ortiz
"Look to the Mountaintop"

The flowers you thanked for their sustaining beauty
that now reconstitute the woods,
the vegetables grown whose woody stalks
are active memories of tactile and nutritious sustenance,
the roadkill laid to the side and blessed,
the aquarium life and death prayed over,
the pleas for the midnight car-crippled doe,
the teenage raccoon worried over to the wildlife care
      center,
the birds fed with religious devotion,
the bird freed from cats and the birds freed by cats,
now buried with a grace,
the wasps captured glass on glass
and released to a hastened fall of inevitable death,
the strays taken in for decades,
the strays taken in for rebirth in better places,
the ladybugs not smashed,
the spiders scooped up on newspaper transports,
the dog you said yes to,
the money you gave so that habitat could still house,
the crickets you watched for in cutting the grass,
the salamanders you re-covered when awakened too early,
the turtles you saved from dog jaws and car wheels,
the trees you killed by their permission
so that their elders might live to tell you tales of survival,
and the wild you have blessed unseen, but not unknown.
When it is your time these are the graces of life
that will greet you there, well, done.

                                        F. Lynne Bachleda

Death is nature's way of telling you to slow down.

1960s life insurance proverb

———

Everything in nature invites us constantly to be what
we are. We are often like rivers: careless and forceful,
timid and dangerous, lucid and muddied, eddying,
gleaming, still. Lovers, farmers, and artists have one
thing in common, at least—a fear of "dry spells,"
dormant periods in which we do no blooming,
internal droughts only the waters of imagination and
psychic release can civilize. All such matters are delicate
of course. But a good irrigator knows this: too little
water brings on the weeds while too much degrades
the soil the way too much easy money can trivialize a
person's initiative. In his journal Thoreau wrote, "A
man's life should be as fresh as a river. It should be the
same channel but a new water every instant."

Gretel Ehrlich
"On Water,"
The Solace of Open Spaces

. . . Those strikes, those recognitions, went on all around me, and though I had traveled far and wide myself I had hardly begun to recognize them; but they come back, if we are on hand to receive them, repeating their directives for our benefit.

There was, for example, the reappearance of my turtle. As a boy, with the wish in me to capture, I kept a painted turtle in a pen, and it surprised me by laying eggs, thus revealing a secret identity. The eggs were eaten by some marauder, though I had desperately wanted to see them hatch out, and later on the turtle died of unknown causes. I suspect it had something to do with mismanaged captivity. I gave it a formal burial under a big sugar maple that stood over a rock wall. I also carved my initials and the date on the plastron, or undershell, of another one. I can still feel the black, low, shiny-smooth, hemispheric shell like a water-worn stone, and the little black legs with clawed feet that felt as soft as the pads on a puppy. Red-orange, yellow, and black are first colors for me. Then, many, many years later, with all kinds of human displacements and holocausts in between, I met it again as it ambled slowly across the grass out in front of that same tree where I had buried its compatriot. And I thanked the turtle as an old friend, not only for the pleasure of meeting it again, but for bringing me back into one of those mutual, lasting circles never stopped by the passage of time. It was like another lease, smelling of apple blossoms in the spring, the way they were and would always be.

John Hay
"Homing,"
The Undisovered Country

Deep peace of the Running Wave to you
Deep peace of the Flowing Air to you
Deep peace of the Quiet Earth to you
Deep peace of the Shining Stars to you
Deep peace of the Gentle Night to you
Deep peace of the Daughters and Sons of Peace to you
Moon and Stars pour their healing light on you
Deep peace to you.

Gaelic blessing

"Years End"

Year's end,
all corners
of this floating world, swept.

Matsuo Basho
Translated by Takashi
Ikemoto & Lucien Stryk

I pray to the birds.
    I pray to the birds because I believe they will carry the messages of my heart upward. I pray to them because I believe in their existence, the way their songs begin and end each day—the invocations and the benedictions of Earth. I pray to the birds because they remind me of what I love rather than what I fear. And at the end of my prayers, they teach me how to listen.

Terry Tempest Williams

We are the miracles that God made
To taste the bitter fruit of Time.
We are precious
And one day our suffering
Will turn into the wonders of the earth . . .

That is why our music is so sweet.
It makes the air remember.
There are secret miracles at work
That only Time will bring forth.
I too have heard the dead singing.

And they tell me that
This life is good
They tell me to live it gently
With fire, and always with hope.
There is wonder here

And there is surprise
In everything the unseen moves.
The ocean is full of songs.
The sky is not an enemy.
Destiny is our friend.

Ben Okri
An African Elegy

SIX

TO RECOGNITION AND COMPASSION

Freed from self-absorption, the move out of self to other

Recognition and compassion sustain the essential goodwill energy of the earth. Imagine seeing ourselves reflected in the seen and unseen eyes of all that surrounds us. Because we have already remembered to look closely, this gentle reflective sanctuary holds all possibilites to apply the golden rule of doing unto others out beyond not only our own kind, but also into the wild frontiers of our dreams.

If you will think of ourselves as coming out of the earth, rather than having been thrown in here from somewhere else, you see that we are the earth, we are the consciousness of the earth. These are the eyes of the earth. And this is the voice of the earth.

Joseph Campbell
The Power of Myth

It was unreasonable to me—this was even before I had gone to school—that in my evening devotions I should pray only for people. So when my mother had prayed with me and kissed me goodnight, I used secretly to add another prayer which I had composed myself for all living creatures. It ran like this: "Dear God, guard and bless everything that breathes; keep them from all evil and let them sleep in peace."

Albert Schweitzer
Reverence for Life:
The Words of Albert Schweitzer

May no living creatures, not even insects,
Be bound into samsaric* life;
nay, not one of them;
But may I be empowered
to save them all.

Milarepa
11–12th century Tibetan saint

Buy captive animals and give them freedom. How
commendable is abstinence that dispenses with the
butcher! While walking be mindful of worms and ants.
Be cautious with fire and do not set mountain woods
or forests ablaze. Do not go into the mountain to catch
birds in nets, nor to the water to poison fishes and
minnows. Do not butcher the ox that plows your field.

Taoist *Tract of the Quiet Way*

* of the "cycle of existence," an endless repetition of birth and
death

What would the world be, once bereft
Of wet and wildness? Let them be left,
O let them be left, wildness and wet;
Long live the weeds and the wilderness yet.

Gerard Manley Hopkins
"Inversnaid"

Whenever a person breaks a stick in the forest, let him
consider what it would feel like, if it were himself that
was thus broken.

Nigerian proverb

Where I stand now, a great tree once grew. The circles that mark the centuries of its life surround me, and I dream back through them. It's difficult to imagine the beginnings—perhaps a seed that fell from a flurry of crossbills like those I saw a while ago. More difficult still is the incomprehensible distance of time this tree crossed, as it grew from a limber switch on the forest floor to a tree perhaps 150 feet tall and weighing dozens of tons. Another way to measure the scope of its life is in terms of storms. Each year scores of them swept down this valley—thousands of boiling gales and blizzards in the tree's lifetime—and it withstood them all.

The man who walked up beside it some twenty years ago would have seemed no more significant than a puff of air on a summer afternoon.

Perhaps thin shafts of light shone down onto the forest floor that day, and danced on the velvet moss. I wonder what that man might have thought, as he looked into the tree's heights and prepared to bring it down. Perhaps he thought only about the job at hand, or his aching back, or how long it was until lunch. I would like to believe he gave some consideration to the tree itself, to its death and his responsibilities toward it, as he pulled the cord that set his chainsaw blaring.

Richard Nelson
The Island Within

[Pythagoras taught] first, that the soul is an immortal thing, and that it is transformed into other kinds of living things; further, that whatever comes into existence is born again in the revolutions of a certain cycle, nothing being absolutely new; and that all things that are born with life in them ought to be treated as kindred.

Peter Marshall
Nature's Web:
Rethinking Our Place on Earth

In order to see much one must learn to look away from oneself—every mountain-climber needs this hardness . . . you must climb above yourself—up and beyond, until you have even your stars under you! Yes! To look down upon myself and even upon my stars: that alone would I call my *summit*, that has remained for me as my *ultimate* summit!

Frederick Nietzsche
Translated by R. J. Hollingdale
Thus Spoke Zarathustra:
A Book for Everyone and No One

One touch of nature makes the whole world kin.

William Shakespeare
Troilus and Cressida, Act III

One evening I find her lying dead beside the road. She has come closer to the houses than usual. The thick hairs are visible among the broken quills. I look closely at her, the clean long gaze that death permits us. Her face is sweet and dark, her inner light replaced by the light of sky. The drifting clouds are in her eyes.

As for me, I have a choice between honoring that dark life I've seen so many years moving in the junipers, or of walking away and going on with my own human busyness. There is always that choice for humans.

I lean over and pick sage and offer it to this animal old woman who lived on earth, who breathed the same air that for years I have been breathing, and that breath prays for all creatures on earth. I remove some quills. I prick my fingers several times, bent there in the dust pulling the sharpness out of death.

By the next morning the porcupine is already sagging. She is nothing but bony angles beneath fur and quill. Her face is gone, and suddenly I notice that the road is alive. Yes, it is moving and alive, and the motion of it surprises me. I turn to look, and the road is full of thousands of fat white maggots. They are leaving the porcupine. The road is an ocean of white. It has a current. Some of the maggots are turning to beetle and flies before they even reach the other side of the road. A wing breaks through here, a black leg there. They lose their white skin, and in their first changing of life, they are crossing the road and are being eaten on the other side by ants that are waiting there.

In that crossing over, that swallowing, the battle of life with life, the porcupine lives on. It lives on in the buzzing of flies and the ants with their organized lives. In its transformation, life continues. My life too, which stopped only for a small moment in history, in the great turning over of the world.

Linda Hogan
"Porcupine,"
Dwellings:
A Spiritual History of the Living World

The jungle hammock breathed. Life went through the moss-hung forest, the swamp, the cypresses, through the wild sow and her young, through me, in its continuous chain. We were all one with the silent pulsing. This was the thing that was important, the cycle of life, with birth and death merging one into the other in an imperceptible twilight and an insubstantial dawn. The universe breathed, and the world inside it breathed the same breath. This was the cosmic life, with suns and moons to make it lovely. It was important only to keep close enough to the pulse to feel its rhythm, to be comforted by its steadiness, to know that Life is vital, and one's own minute living a torn fragment of the larger cloth.

Marjorie Kinnan Rawlings
"The Magnolia Tree,"
Cross Creek

"I Live My Life in Widening Circles"

I live my life in widening circles
that reach out across the world.
I may not complete this last one
but I give myself to it.

I circle around God, around the primordial tower.
I've been circling for thousands of years
and I still don't know: am I a falcon,
a storm, or a great song?

Rainer Maria Rilke
Translated by Anita Barrows & Joanna Macy
Rilke's Book of Hours: Love Poems to God

Up high all the birds have flown away,
A single cloud drifts off across the sky.
We settle down together, never tiring of each other,
Only the two of us, the mountain and I.

Li Po
8th century Taoist poet

I once spent a summer day at the mountain home of a well-known literary woman and editor. She lamented the absence of birds about her house. I named a half-dozen or more I had heard or seen in her trees within an hour—the indigo-bird, the purple finch, the yellowbird, the veery thrush, the red-eyed vireo, the song sparrow.

"Do you mean to say you have seen or heard all these birds while sitting here on my porch?" she inquired.

"I really have," I said.

"I do not see them or hear them," she replied, "and yet I want to very much."

"No," said I; "you only *want to want* to see and hear them."

You must have the bird in your heart before you can find it in the bush.

John Burroughs
"The Art of Seeing Things"

"A Doe at Evening"

As I went through the marshes
a doe sprang up out of the corn
and flashed up the hill-side
leaving her fawn.

On the sky-line
she moved round to watch,
she pricked a fine blotch
on the sky.

I looked at her
and felt her watching;
I became a strange being.
Still, I had my right to be there with her.
Her nimble shadow trotting
along the sky-line, she
put back her fine, level-balanced head.
And I knew her.

Ah yes, being male, is not my head hard-balanced,
    antlered?
Are not my haunches light?
Has she not fled on the same wind with me?
Does not my fear cover her fear?

D. H. Lawrence

One day I took a walk near my island home. Across the road a rufous doe grazed in the meadow with her new fawn—a picture of docility. A large yellow dog sauntered down the road toward me. He was bulky and intimidating, even from a distance. He stopped at the edge of the road to watch the doe and her fawn in the meadow. The fawn went on munching grass. The doe glanced up at the big dog, and then continued grazing. As I neared the dog, the fawn moved a few feet away from its mother. The dog sized up the scene very carefully. The moment he saw a beeline between himself and the fawn, he shot toward it at lightning speed. I shouted, as if that would stop him, but my voice mattered little. For a brief second it looked as if the fawn would be done for, and then I saw the rufous doe behave as I'd never seen before. She raised up tall and filled her chest with air, magnifying her size. She swiftly positioned herself between the dog and her fawn. Then she directly faced the dog. I feared he'd go for her throat and take her down, but no. Instead he hesitated before her. Then she advanced toward him stomping like a flamenco dancer. Her sharp black hooves pummeled the earth. It was quite impressive. At this the dog retreated. I hoped that would be the end of it. He left them in the meadow and returned to the road. I shooed him and commanded, "Go home!" But he was still intrigued.

He stayed there at the road's edge, eyeing the deer, waiting for another opening. The doe seemed as casual as could be. She grazed without looking up. She allowed the fawn to wander. She could surely hear me shooing the dog, but she seemed to pay us no mind. At last the dog saw his chance. He darted across the field toward the fawn. The fawn seemed oblivious, but the doe moved more fleetly than before. In an instant she was protectively positioned to guard her fawn. She reared up to show the dog her height. Then she advanced toward him, hammering her hooves in his face, mincing the grass at her feet. He moved backward a few steps. She kept pounding. Her hooves could easily have gouged out his eye or punctured his chest. But she seemed to want to demonstrate the threat of it without actually doing the damage. He turned tail and ran several feet as he had done before. But this time she kept coming, tearing up the sod beneath her hooves as she advanced. The dog ran to the road, then turned around to watch her. She held her ground at the edge of the road. He lowered his head to threaten another advance, and she puffed up and thumped the earth again as if to say, "Just try it, Buster." It was daunting, this dance of hers. The dog wanted no more of it and skulked away down the road.

Since then I've concluded the rufous doe is a superb model for any woman. Her gentle calm is appropriate for nearly every situation, except the rare occasions when salivating jaws threaten. Then it's necessary to have a set of sharp hooves up one's sleeve and the resolve to keep stomping until the predator retreats.

When people praise doe-eyed gentleness, I don't argue, but I'll never forget she can be every bit as fierce as she is soft.

Since then, when life brings me face-to-face with a predator, my knees still knock and my legs tremble. But now I know this is more than a reflex, more than just fear. It's the dance of the deer stirring inside—it's my hooves warming up—preparing to stomp.

Erica Helm Meade
"Dance of the Deer"

Every part of this soil is sacred in the estimation of my people. Every hillside, every valley, every plain and grove, has been hallowed by some sad or happy event in days long vanished. The very dust upon which you now stand responds more lovingly to their footsteps than to yours, because it is rich with the blood of our ancestors and our bare feet are conscious of the sympathetic touch. Even the little children who live here and rejoiced here for a brief season will love these somber solitudes and at eventide they greet shadowy returning spirits.

Chief Sealth
19th century Duwamish
Native American

If we have a wonderful sense of the divine, it is because we live amid such awesome magnificence. If we have refinement of emotion and sensitivity, it is because of the delicacy, the fragrance, and indescribable beauty of song and music and rhythmic movement in the world about us. If we grow in our life vigor, it is because the earthly community challenges us, forces us to struggle to survive, but in the end reveals itself as a benign providence. But however benign, it must provide that absorbing drama of existence whereby we can experience the thrill of being alive in a fascinating and unending sequence of adventures.

If we have powers of imagination, these are activated by the magic display of color and sound, of form and movement, such as we observe in the clouds of the sky, the trees and bushes and flowers, the waters and the wind, the singing birds, and the movement of the great blue whale through the sea. If we have words with which to speak and think and commune, words for the inner experience of the divine, words for the intimacies of life, if we have words for telling stories to our children, words with which we can sing, it is again because of the impressions we have received from the variety of beings about us.

Thomas Berry
The Dream of the Earth

Folks who laugh and say that all is known about Nature, and that Nature don't have a soul-spirit, have never been in a mountain spring storm. When She's birthing spring, She gets right down to it, tearing at the mountains like a birthing woman clawing at the bed quilts.

If a tree has been hanging on, having weathered all the winter winds, and She figures it needs cleaning out, She whips it up out of the ground and flings it down the mountain. She goes over the branches of every bush and tree, and after She feels around a little with Her wind fingers, then She whips them clean and proper of anything that is weak.

If She figures a tree needs removing and won't come down from the wind, She just whams! and all that's left is a torch blazing from a lightning stroke. She's alive and paining. You'll believe it too.

Forrest Carter
The Education of Little Tree

Don't you realize that the sea is the home of water? All water is off on a journey unlessen it's in the sea, and it's homesick, and bound to make its way home someday.

Zora Neale Hurston
Seraph on the Suwanee

"Page from a Journal"

On the slope behind the house today
I cut through roots and rocks and
Dug a hole, deep and wide,
Carted away from it each stone
And all the friable, thin earth.
Then I knelt there a moment, walked
In the old woods, bent down again, using
A trowel and both my hands to scoop
Black, decaying woods-soil with the warm
Smell of fungi from the trunk of a rotting
Chestnut tree—two heavy buckets full I carried
Back to the hole and planted the tree inside;
Carefully I covered the roots with peaty soil,
Slowly poured sun-warmed water over them,
Mudding them gently until the soil settled.
It stands there, young and small,
Will go on standing when we are gone
And the huge uproar, endless urgency and
Fearful delirium of our days forgotten.

The föhn* will bend it, rainstorms tear at it,
The sun will laugh, wet snow weigh it down,
The siskin and the nuthatch make it their home,
And the silent hedgehog burrow at its foots.
All it has ever experienced, tasted, suffered:

* warm southerly wind

The course of years, generations of animals,
Oppression, recovery, friendship of sun and wind
Will pour forth each day in the song
Of its rustling foliage, in the friendly
Gesture of its gently swaying crown,
In the delicate sweet scent of resinous
Sap moistening the sleep-glued buds,
And in the eternal game of lights and
Shadow it plays with itself, content.

Hermann Hesse
Translated by Rika Lesser
Hours in the Garden and Other Poems

———

God is the friend of silence. See how nature—trees,
flowers, grass—grows in silence; see the stars, the moon
and the sun, how they move in silence. . . . We need
silence to be able to touch souls.

Mother Teresa

Nature, like man, sometimes weeps for gladness.

Benjamin Disraeli

 Let's talk of graves, of worms, of epitaphs;
Make dust our paper and with rainy eyes
Write sorrow on the bosom of the earth.
Let's choose our executors, and talk of wills. . . .
For God's sake, let us sit upon the ground
And tell sad stories of the death of kings.

William Shakespeare
Richard II, Act III

. . . I was away from the shellers now and strode more rapidly over the wet sand that effaced my footprints. Around the next point there might be a refuge from the wind. The sun behind me was pressing upward at the horizon's rim—an ominous red glare amidst the tumbling blackness of the clouds. Ahead of me, over the projecting point, a gigantic rainbow of incredible perfection had sprung shimmering into existence. Somewhere toward its foot I discerned a human figure standing, as it seemed to me, within the rainbow, though unconscious of his position. He was gazing fixedly at something in the sand.

Eventually he stooped and flung the object beyond the breaking surf. I labored toward him over a half-mile of uncertain footing. By the time I reached him the rainbow had receded ahead of us, but something of its color still ran hastily in many changing lights across his features. He was starting to kneel again.

In a pool of sand and silt a starfish had thrust its arms up stiffly and was holding its body away from the stifling mud.

"It's still alive," I ventured.

"Yeah," he said, and with a quick yet gentle movement he picked up the star and spun it over my head and far out into the sea. It sank in a burst of spume, and the waters roared once more.

"It may live," he said, "if the offshore pull is strong enough." He spoke gently, and across his bronzed worn face the light still came and went in subtly altering colors.

"There are not many come this far," I said, groping in a sudden embarrassment for words. "Do you collect?"

"Only like this," he said softly, gesturing amidst the wreckage of the shore. "And only for the living." He stooped again, oblivious of my curiosity, and skipped another star neatly across the water.

"The stars," he said, "throw well. One can help them."

He looked full at me with a faint question kindling in his eyes, which seemed to take on the far depths of the sea. . . .

Man is himself, like the universe he inhabits, like the demoniacal stirrings of the ooze from which he sprang, a tale of desolations. He walks in his mind from birth to death the long resounding shores of endless disillusionment. Finally, the commitment to life departs or turns to bitterness. But out of such desolation emerges the awesome freedom to choose—to choose beyond the narrowly subscribed circle that delimits the animal being. In that widening ring of human choice, chaos and order renew their symbolic struggle in the role of titans. They contend for the destiny of a world. . . .

On a point of land, as though projecting into a domain beyond us, I found the star thrower. In the sweet rain-swept morning, that great many-hued rainbow still lurked and waived tentatively beyond him. Silently I sought and picked up a still-living star, spinning it far out into the waves. I spoke [to him] once briefly. "I understand," I said. "Call me another thrower." Only then I allowed myself to think, he is not alone any longer. After us there will be others.

We were part of the rainbow—an unexplained projection into the natural. As I went down the beach I could feel the drawing of a circle in men's minds, like that lowering, shifting realm of color in which the thrower labored. It was a visible model of something toward which man's mind had striven, the circle of perfection.

I picked and flung another star. Perhaps far outward on the rim of space a genuine star was similarly seized and flung. I could feel the movement in my body. It was like a sowing—the sowing of life on an infinitely gigantic scale. I looked back across my shoulder. Small and dark against the receding rainbow, the star thrower stood and flung once more. I never looked again. The task we had assumed was too immense for gazing. I flung and flung again while all about us roared the insatiable waters of death.

Loren Eiseley
"The Star Thrower"
The Unexpected Universe

But the old woman merely looked at them and said, "To be human is to be born, partake of life, and die. Life itself is the gift. It does not have to be wrenched out of shape, trying to deny both the borning and the dying. Women produce children, and they and the children die. But they know that it was good to have lived. Perhaps someday men too can rest upon the affirmation of being, and there find reassurance and an end to their ceaseless striving. Perhaps someday they shall come to know the circle which is the whole—that which validates being-without-achieving, that which allows one to rest and stop running, that which accepts one as a person and not a hero. The sweet nectar of that whole awaits you in the precious flower of the Now, not in your dreams of glory. Perhaps, someday, men will find their humanity, and give up their divinity."

The old woman had finished speaking and there was silence in the great council room. It was a time for silence.

Elizabeth Dodson Gray
"Turning to Another Way,"
Green Paradise Lost

SEVEN

TO HOPE, RESOLVE,
AND BEYOND

With a soul newly restored, the call to return

Hope and and her resulting partner resolve are renewable resources. Nature never runs out of hope. The challenge is to build a nest, a bear's den, a bramble of thicket to hold in the hope accumulated along the journey's way. Every rocket rider plans for re-entry. If you're not sure how much hope you've got at home, better stop off again and fill up your tank. Hope: just ask for it by name.

155

None of our former revelatory experiences, none of our renewal or rebirth rituals, none of our apocalyptic descriptions are quite adequate for this moment. Their mythic power remains in a context far removed from the power that is abroad in our world. But even as we glance over the grimy world before us, the sun shines radiantly over the earth, the aspen leaves shimmer in the evening breeze, the coo of the mourning dove and the swelling chorus of the insects fill the land, while down in the hollows the mist deepens the fragrance of the honeysuckle. Soon the late summer moon will give a light sheen to the landscape. Something of a dream experience. Perhaps on occasion we participate in the original dream of the earth. Perhaps there are times when this primordial design becomes visible, as in a palimpsest, when we remove the later imposition. The dream of the earth. Where else can we go for the guidance needed for the task that is before us.

Thomas Berry
The Dream of the Earth

Today, now, this moment,
I promise myself to reach out and touch the earth.
I will dig my fingers into the soil and remember what
    it is that sustains me.

It is not wealth.
It is not possessions.
It is not achievements.
It is not the praise of men.

It is this that I touch, the sacred soil, the fertile field,
    the living land, the holy.

Today, now, this moment,
I promise myself to reach out and touch a fellow
    creature.
I will run my hand along fur, feathers, shell, or scales
    and remember what sustains him.

It is not wealth.
It is not possessions.
It is not achievements.
It is not the praise of men.

It is the ocean eternal, the infinite sky, the sun, the
    rain, the holy earth.

Today, now, this moment.

I promise myself to reach out and embrace
    understanding.

I will hold to my breast the reality that my fellow
    creatures and I are equals in the Mother's love.

It is not wealth.

It is not possessions.

It is not achievements.

It is not the praise of men.

It is food and breath, life and death, the stars above us
    and the holy earth.

Laurel Olson

We have forgotten what we can count on. The natural world provides refuge. . . . Each of us harbors a homeland, a landscape we naturally comprehend. By understanding the dependability of place, we can anchor ourselves as trees.

One night, Jonas Ole Sademaki, a Maasai elder, and I sit around the fire telling stories. Sparks enter the ebony sky and find their places among stars.

"My people worship trees," he says. "It was the tree that gave birth to the Maasai. Grasses are also trustworthy. When a boy is beaten for an inappropriate act, the boy falls to the ground and clutches a handful of grass. His elder takes this gesture as a sign of humility. The child remembers where the source of his power lies."

As I walk back to my tent, I stop and look up at the southern cross. These are new constellations for me. I kneel in the grasses and hold tight.

Terry Tempest Williams
"In the Country of Grasses"

So we are engaged in an ongoing struggle, a search for a new relation to the earth. It is also an old relationship: to be in and of place, to truly inhabit the land rather than just live on it. Why is it important? The answer is all around us in the destruction of habitats, species, and individual beings, often done out of ignorance, greed, and fear. The answer is also inside us, in a psychological rupture from the physical matrix of our life—nature and our bodies. And the answer is in the way we treat each other: our debasement and abuse of nature is linked with our debasement and abuse of people. To heal the social and the psychological, we need to heal our relationship with the earth. And vice versa. As Buddhism teaches, all of life is a mutual co-arising: everything conditions and is conditioned by everything else.

David Landis Barnhill
"Introduction,"
At Home on the Earth:
Becoming Native to Our Place,
A Multicultural Anthology

The politics of place is a politics of hope. It is sustained by a faith—somewhat mystical perhaps—in *place* itself. Whether they are descendants of Asian hunters who crossed the Bering land bridge during the Ice Age or mongrels with New England Puritan Irish-Polish-Jewish blood, all people who put down roots are shaped by their home ground. Over time it seeps into them, and they become natives. In the Northwest this means they look up at twilight and draw strength from the mountains. They seek renewal at the rivers and the shores. They taste communion in the pink flesh of the salmon. The rains cease to annoy.

Here is the hope: that this generation becomes the next wave of natives, first in this place on Earth and then in others. That newfound permanence allows the quiet murmur of localities to become audible again. And that not long thereafter, perhaps very soon, the places of this Earth will be healed and whole again.

From Port Arthur in British Columbia, maverick timber boss A. J. Auden of the Abitibi Power and Paper Company had it right fifty years ago when he said, "We have spent the past two hundred and fifty years . . . in restless movement, recklessly skimming off the cream of superabundant resources, but we have not used the land in the true sense of the word, nor have we done ourselves much permanent good. It's high time that we . . . settled down, not for a hundred years, but a thousand, forever."

Alan Thein Durning
This Place on Earth:
Home and the Practice of Permanence

—————

None of us can predict or control the career or avocational choices of our children. All we can do is introduce, try to prevent prejudice, battle gender stereotypes, teach by the example of our own attention and wonder. All we can do is recite from the Scripture of maps and field guides. Give names to the mountains and rivers, give names to the trees. Give voice to the emotions that storms and tundra flowers, young bison and soaring ravens can pull from us.

As parents, we can take our children with us to the land. We can be there with them as they climb on rocks, play in streams and waves, dig in the rich soil of woods and gardens, putter and learn. Here, on the land, we learn from each other. Here, our children's journey begins.

Stephen Trimble
Words from the Land:
Encounters with Natural History Writing

Mountains help us to regain that sense of freshness and wonder possessed by a child. They awaken us to a deeper reality hidden in the world around us, even in cities, far from the sight of the peaks themselves. Moved by the mysterious power of this hidden reality, we recover the vision and delight of childhood, enhanced by the experience and understanding of age. Eyes bright and clear, hearts open and free, we stand once again at the beginning and source of all that is and all that may be.

Edwin Bernbaum
Sacred Mountains of the World

I used to have a cat, an old fighting tom, who would jump through the open window by my bed in the middle of the night and land on my chest. I'd half-awaken. He'd stick his skull under my nose and purr, stinking of urine and blood. Some nights he kneaded my bare chest with his front paws, powerfully, arching his back, as if sharpening his claws, or pummeling a mother for milk. And some mornings I'd wake in daylight to find my body covered with paw prints in blood; I looked as though I'd been painted with roses.

It was hot, so hot the mirror felt warm. I washed before the mirror in a daze, my twisted summer sleep still hung about me like sea kelp. What blood was this, and what roses? It could have been the rose of union, the blood of murder, or the rose of beauty bare and the blood of some unspeakable sacrifice or birth. The sign on my body could have been an emblem or a stain, the keys to the kingdom or the mark of Cain. I never knew. I never knew as I washed, and the blood streaked, faded, and finally disappeared, whether I'd purified myself or ruined the blood sign of the passover. We wake, if we ever wake at all, to mystery, rumors of death, beauty, violence . . . "Seem like we're just set down here," a woman said to me recently, "and don't nobody know why."

These are morning matters, pictures you dream as the final wave heaves you up on the sand to the bright light and drying air. You remember pressure, and a curved sleep you rested against, soft, like a scallop in its shell. But the air hardens your skin; you stand; you leave the lighted shore to explore some dim headland, and soon you're lost in the leafy interior, intent, remembering nothing.

I still think of that old tomcat, mornings, when I wake. Things are tamer now; I sleep with the window shut. The cat and our rites are gone and my life is changed, but the memory remains of something powerful playing over me. I wake expectant, hoping to see a new thing.

Annie Dillard
"Heaven and Earth in Jest,"
Pilgrim at Tinker Creek

When I climb I almost always carry seeds with me in my pocket. Often I like to carry sunflower seeds, or an acorn, or any queer "sticktight" that has a way of gripping fur or boot tops as if it had a deliberate eye on the Himalayas and meant to use the intelligence of others to arrive at them. More than one lost mountaineer lying dead at the bottom of a crevasse has proved that his sole achievement in life was to inch some plant a half-mile further toward the moon. His body may have been scarcely cold before that illicit transported seed had been getting a foothold beneath him on a patch of stony ground or writhing its way into a firm engagement with the elements on the moisture of his life's blood. I have carried such seeds up the sheer walls of mesas and I have never had illusions that I was any different to them than a grizzly's back or a puma's paw. . . .

Life is never fixed and stable. It is always mercurial, rolling and splitting, disappearing and reemerging in a quite bewildering fashion. It is constantly changing, and now it has affected me to the extent that I never make a journey to a wood or a mountain without the temptation to explode a puffball in a new clearing or encourage some sleepy monster that is just cracking out of the earth mold. It is, of course, an irresponsible attitude, since I cannot tell what will come of it. No doubt man himself may have been the indirect product of a tumbleweed blowing past the eyes of a curious primate hanging poised from a bough to which he forgot to climb back after he had chased the weed out into the grass. Naturally this is a simplification, but if the world hangs on such matters it may be as well to act boldly and realize all immanent possibilities at once. Shake the seeds out of their pods, launch the milkweed down, and set the lizards scuttling. We are in a creative universe. Let us then create.

Loren Eiseley
"Evolution Can Be Seen,"
The Lost Notebooks of Loren Eiseley

In the ordinary course of nature, the great beneficent changes come slowly and silently. The noisy changes, for the most part, mean violence and disruption. The roar of storms and tornadoes, the explosions of volcanoes, the crash of the thunder are the result of a sudden break in the equipoise of the elements; from a condition of comparative repose and silence they become fearfully swift and audible. The still small voice is the voice of life and growth and perpetuity. In the stillness of a bright summer day what work is being accomplished, what processes are being consummated! . . . The great loom in which is woven all the living clothe[s] the world with verdure and people[s] it with animated forms [and] makes no sound.

John Buroughs
"The Still Small Voice"

So we saunter toward the Holy Land, till one day the sun shall shine more brightly than ever he has done, shall perchance shine into our minds and hearts, and light up our whole lives with a great awakening light, as warm and serene and golden as on a bankside in autumn.

Henry David Thoreau
"Walking"

"Autumn Burns Me"

Autumn burns me with
primaeval fire. Makes my skin
taut with expectation,
hurls me out of summer fatigue
on to a new Bridge of Sighs.

Somewhere I feel the heart
of the earth pumping, and down below
it bleeds in a million ripples.
I drop a sweet memory into
the flow and the cascading grips me with fascination

Great trees in transit fall
are made naked in languor of shame
solitary like actors on a stage

like stars, orphans, celebrities,
politicians, uncomfortably mysteriously like
    you and me.

But I will not mourn the sadness.
I will go dead-leaf gathering
for the fire in a slice of sunlight
to fill my lungs with odours of decay
and my eyes with mellowed rainbow colours

I will go creeping down tasselled
latticed tree-avenues of light
and listen to squirrel tantrums
punctuate the orchestration of autumn silence
and hold in my hand the coiling stuff of nature

Then I will love
Yes love; extravagantly under
the flutter of dying leaves
and in a shadow of mist
in wonder; for autumn is wonder and wonder is hope.

Lenrie Peters
a West African poet

And it shall come to pass in the end of days,
That the mountain of the Lord's house shall be
established as the top of the mountains,
And shall be exalted above the hills;
And all nations shall flow unto it.
And many peoples shall go and say:
'Come ye, and let us go up to the mountain of
    the Lord,
To the house of the God of Jacob;
And He will teach us of His ways,
And we will walk in His paths.'
For out of Zion shall go forth the law,
And the word of the Lord from Jerusalem.
And He shall judge between the nations,
And shall decide for many peoples;
And they shall beat their swords into plowshares,
And their spears into pruning-hooks;
Nation shall not lift up sword against nation,
    either shall they learn war any more.

Isaiah 2:2–4

Some have named this space where we are rooted
a place of death.
We fix them with our callous eyes
and call it, rather, a terrain of resurrection.

Robin Morgan
"Easter Island, I: Embarcation,"
Monster

Like winds and sunsets, wild things were taken for
granted until progress began to do away with them.
Now we face the question whether a still higher
"standard of living" is worth its cost in things natural,
wild, and free. For us of the minority, the opportunity
to see geese is more important than television, and the
chance to find a pasque-flower is a right as inalienable
as free speech.

Aldo Leopold
A Sand County Almanac

But that land—it is one thing that will still be there when I come back—land is always there. . . .

Pearl S. Buck
A House Divided

The teeth at your bones are your own, the hunger is yours, forgiveness is yours. The sins of the fathers belong to you and to the forest and even to the ones in iron bracelets, and here you stand, remembering their songs. Listen. Slide the weight from your shoulders and move forward. You are afraid you might forget, but you never will. You will forgive and remember. Think of the vine that curls from the small square plot that was once my heart. That is the only marker you need. Move on. Walk forward into the light.

Barbara Kingsolver
The Poisonwood Bible

... that Blue [of the sky] ... will always be there as it is now after all man's destruction is finished.

Georgia O'Keeffe

"God's Grandeur"

The world is charged with the grandeur of God.
   It will flame out, like shining from shook foil;
   It gathers to a greatness, like the ooze of oil
Crushed.[1] Why do men then now not reck[2] his rod?
Generations have trod, have trod, have trod;
   And all is seared with trade; bleared, smeared with toil;
   And wear's man's smudge and share's man's smell:
      the soil
Is bare now, nor can foot feel, being shod.

And for all this, nature is never spent;
   There lives the dearest freshness deep down things;
And though the last lights of the the black West went
   Oh, morning, at the brown brink eastward, springs—
Because the Holy Ghost over the bent
   World broods with warm breast and with ah!
      bright wings.

Gerard Manley Hopkins

[1] as from olives
[2] to care for; regard

God, in Your form of Beauty be with us.

May our hearts be broken. May our prayers be sufficient to feel the heartbreak of God.

God is not steel or any of the indestructible alloys we have created. God is a block of granite that stretches up from deep in the earth to the sky. God is the same stone etched by two white rivulets we call Current and Waterfall, flowing endlessly, carving the right and left hands whose names are also Beauty and Sorrow so that every drop rives the four chambers of the great heart. This is eternal. The Rising and the Falling. The Salt and the Sweet. The Burn and the Poultice. The Division and the Communion.

It never ceases: Dismay and Hope, Agony and Forgiveness. These are the four directions that Sun and Moon mark for us and that Day and Night illuminate. This is what we call East, West, North, South, thinking we can walk one way or another and not succumb to Windstorm, Earthquake, Volcano, or Drowning.

We want to be God in all the ways that are not the ways of God, in what we hope is indestructible or unmoving. But God is the most fragile, a bare smear of pollen, that scatter of yellow dust from the tree that tumbled over in a storm of grief and planted itself again. God is the death agony of the frog that cannot find water in the time of the drought of our creation. God is the scream of the rabbit caught in the fires we set. God is the One whose eyes never close and who hears everything.

Even if nothing can be fixed, let the vision reconstitute us through a pinhole in time and space—a vision of the lonely God carrying the burden of universal sorrow. Let us take Her in our arms. Let us stroke His temples.

These are our tasks. Let us learn the secret languages of light again. Also the letters of the dark. Learn the flight patterns of birds, the syllables of wolf howl and bird song, the moving pantomime of branch and leaf, valleys and peaks of whale calls, the long sentences of ants moving in unison, the combinations and recombinations of clouds, the codices of stars. Let us, thus, reconstitute the world, sign by sign and melody by melody

Let us sing the world back into the very Heart of the Holy Name of God.

Deena Metzger

"Demeter"

In your dream you met Demeter
Splendid and severe, who said: Endure.
Study the art of seeds,
The nativity of caves.
Dance your gay body to the poise of waves;
Die out of the world to bring forth the obscure
Into blisses, into needs.
In all resources
Belong to love. Bless,
Join, fashion the deep forces.
Asserting your nature, priceless and feminine.
Peace, daughter. Find your true kin.
  —then you felt her kiss.

Genevieve Taggard
Slow Music

Future myths will be different from past myths, but their function will be the same—to sustain life. When the human element was small, when there were billions of trees and only thousands of people, it was sustaining to imagine that trees contained spirits humans could talk to, propitiate, befriend. It gave proportion to the world. Now, when there are billions of people, and not so many trees, it is sustaining to imagine what it might be like to open one's flowers on a spring afternoon, or to stand silently, making food out of sunlight, for a thousand years. It gives proportion to the world.

David Rains Wallace
The Klamath Knot

One early morning last spring, I came and found the woods floor strewn with bluebells. In the cool sunlight and the lacy shadows of the spring woods the blueness of those flowers, their elegant shape, their delicate fresh scent kept me standing and looking. I found a rich delight in them that I cannot describe and that I will never forget. Though I had been familiar for years with most of the spring woods flowers, I had never seen these and had not known they grew here. Looking at them, I felt a strange feeling of loss and sorrow that I had never seen them before. But I was also exultant that I saw them now—that they were here.

For me, in the thought of them will always be the sense of the joyful surprise with which I found them— the sense that came suddenly to me then that the world is blessed beyond my understanding, more abundantly than I will ever know. What lives are still ahead of me here to be discovered and exulted in, tomorrow, or in twenty years? What wonder will be found here on the morning after my death? Though as a man I inherit great evils and the possibility of great loss and suffering, I know that my life is blessed and graced by the yearly flowering of the bluebells. How perfect they are! In their presence I am humble and joyful. If I were given all the learning and all the methods of my race I could not make one of them, or even imagine one. Solomon in all his glory was not arrayed like one of these. It is the privilege and the labor of the apprentice of creation to come with his imagination into the unimaginable, and with his speech into the unspeakable.

Wendell Berry
"A Native Hill,"
Recollected Essays 1965–1980

I prefer winter and fall, when you feel the bone structure of the landscape—the loneliness of it—the dead feeling of winter. Something waits beneath it—the whole story doesn't show.

Andrew Wyeth

Walking here in the middle,
it comes to me again
how much I love the tangled woods,
and how grateful I am
for the path proceeding through them.

F. Lynne Bachleda

In the depth of winter, I finally learned that within me there lay an invincible summer.

Albert Camus

Man's real nature is primarily spiritual life, which weaves its threads of mind to build a cocoon of flesh, encloses its own soul in the cocoon, and, for the first time, the spirit becomes flesh. Understand this clearly: the cocoon is not the silkworm; in the same way, they physical body is not man but merely man's cocoon. Just as the silkworm will break out of its cocoon and fly free, so, too, will man break out of his body-cocoon and ascend to the spiritual world when his time is come. Never think that the death of the physical body is the death of man. Since man is life, he will never know death.

Seicho-No-Ie
Nectarean Shower of Holy Doctrines

To every thing there is a season, and a time to every
   purpose under the heaven:
A time to be born, and a time to die:
A time to plant, and a time to pluck up that which is
   planted;
A time time kill and a time to heal; a time to break
   down, and a time to build up;
A time to weep, and a time to laugh; a time to mourn,
   and a time to dance;
A time to cast away stones, and a time to gather stones
   together; a time to embrace, and a time to refrain
   from embracing;
A time to get and a time to lose; a time to keep, and a
   time to cast away;
A time to rend, and a time to sew; a time to keep
   silence, and a time to speak;
A time to love, and a time to hate; a time of war, and a
   time of peace.

Solomon
Ecclesiastes 3:1–8

The fish trap exists because of the fish; once you've gotten the fish, you can forget the trap. The rabbit snare exists because of the rabbit; once you've gotten the rabbit, you can forget the snare. Words exist because of meaning; once you've gotten the meaning, you can forget the words. Where can I find a man who has forgotten words so I can have a word with him?

Chuang-Tzu
4th century B.C.E. Taoist sage

I slept outdoors last night because I could not bear to go in. The cabin, which only last winter seemed cozy and inviting, has begun to seem stuffy and limiting, so I spread a piece of plastic on the ground to keep off the damp, put my sleeping bag on it and dropped off to sleep watching the stars. [My dog] Tazzie likes to be near me, and with me on the ground. . . .

We have Time, or at least the awareness of it. We have lived long enough and seen enough to understand in a more than intellectual way that we will die, and so we have learned to live as though we are mortal, making our decisions with care and thought because we will not be able to make them again. Time for us will have an end; it is precious, and we have learned its value. . . . Because our culture has assigned us no real role, we can make up our own. It is a good time to be a grown-up woman with individuality, strength and crotchets. We are wonderfully free. We live long. Our children are the independent adults we helped them to become, and though they may still want our love they do not need our care. Social rules are so flexible today that nothing we do is shocking. There are no political barriers to us anymore. Provided we stay healthy and can support ourselves, we can do anything, have anything and spend our talents any way that we please. . . .

That is why I have stopped sleeping inside. A house is too small, too confining. I want the whole world, and the stars too.

Sue Hubbell
"Becoming Feral,"
A Country Year: Living the Questions

Lie quietly along the earth
That sky may send its strength through you
Into the spinning planet.
Absorb from eons of tumultuous change
The rhythms pulsing up through fire and water,
    rock and roots of growing things,
Your body filtering with flesh and spirit
Earth's vibrant offering to the sky.
You are the instrument of peace,
The promise of renewal to a time and place
    not of your body
But dependent on your willingness to give yourself
    to earth and sky;
To make belief in goodness shape a thousand years to
    come
May blessings be your gift, both given and received.

Great spirit, father of us all,
Dear mother earth,
Combine your might
And use our love
To make this body whole,
For now and forever.

Judith Billings

Here is the test to find whether your mission on earth is finished. If you're alive, it isn't.

Richard Bach

———

You are all so much alive. So different. . . . You are a strange species, not like any other. Shall I tell you what I find beautiful about you? You are at your very best when things are worst.

From the motion picture *Starman*
screenplay by Bruce A. Evans
& Raynold Gideon

"When You Wish Upon a Star"

When you wish upon a star,
makes no diff'rence who you are,
Anything your heart desires will come to you.
If your heart is in your dream,
no request is too extreme.
When you wish upon a star as dreamers do.

Fate is kind,
She brings to those who love,
the sweet fulfillment of their secret longing.
Like a bolt out of the blue,
Fate steps in and sees you thru.
When you wish upon a star your dream comes true.

Ned Washington
Walt Disney's *Pinnochio*
used by permission from Bourne Co.

"The hour is striking so close above me"

The hour is striking so close above me,
so clear and sharp,
that all my senses ring with it.
I feel it now: there's a power in me
to grasp and give shape to my world.

I know that nothing has ever been real
without my beholding it.
All becoming has needed me.
My looking ripens things
and they come toward me, to meet and be met.

Rainer Maria Rilke
Translated by Anita Barrows & Joanna Macy
Rilke's Book of Hours: Love Poems to God

———

Starry nights, moonlit nights, with the sea in the distance,
its tremendous gravity poised beyond us, its waves belting
the shore. If I know that Cancer the crab scuttles across
the tidal flats to its designated part of the sky; if I know
Pisces the fish swims off light-years away, I too can follow, from one home to another. To be head-taut with the
stars around you, foot secure on soil and stone, to know
your direction and return through outer signs, is as new
as it is ancient. We are still people of the planet, with all
its original directions waiting in our being.

John Hay
"Homing," *The Undiscovered Country*

I see [bats] through human eyes that turn around a vision, eyes that see the world upside down before memory rights it. I don't hear the high-pitched language of their living, don't know if they have sorrow or if they tell stories longer than a rainstorm's journey, but I see them. How can we get there from here, I wonder, to the center of the world, to the place where the universe carries down the song of night to our human lives. How can we listen or see to find our way by feel to the heart of every yes or no? How do we learn to trust ourselves enough to hear the chanting of earth? To know what's alive or absent around us, and penetrate the void behind our eyes, the old, slow pulse of things, until a wild flying wakes up in us, a new mercy climbs out and takes wing in the sky?

Linda Hogan
"The Bats,"
Dwellings: A Spiritual History
of the Living World

I think over again my small adventures,
My fears,
Those small ones that seemed so big,
For all the vital things
I had to get and reach;
And yet there is only one great thing,
The only thing,
To live to see the great day that dawns
And the light that fills the world.

19th century Inuit Native American

CODA

Why, you ask, do I live up in these blue mountains?
I smile and do not reply. Leave me in peace.
Peach blossoms drift on waves of flowing water,
There is another sky, another earth, beyond the world of men.

Li Po
8th century Taoist poet

ACKNOWLEDGMENTS

The compiler and publisher gratefully acknowledge the following sources for permission to use copyrighted material and for their cooperation in fair use and public domain applications. Every effort has been made to trace copyright holders, and the publisher would be grateful to hear from any copyright holders not acknowledged.

Alternate Arthur Waley translation of coda poem by Li Po: *You asked me what my reason is for lodging in the grey hills, / I smiled but made no reply, for my thoughts were idling on their own; / Like the flowers of the peach-tree borne by the stream, they had sauntered far away / To other climes, to other lands that are not in the World of Men.*

Abbey, Edward. Reprinted by permission of Don Congdon Associates, Inc. Copyright © 1968 by Edward Abbey, renewed 1996 by Clarke Abbey.

Ackerman, Diane. From *A Natural History of the Senses* by Diane Ackerman. Copyright © 1990 by Diane Ackerman. Reprinted by permission of Random House, Inc.

Adams, Ansel. From *Ansel Adams: An Autobiography*. Copyright © 1985 Ansel Adams. Published by Little

Berlin. © Copyright Renewed. International copyright secured. All rights reserved. Reprinted by permission.

Berry, Thomas. From *The Dream of Earth* by Thomas Berry. Copyright © 1990 by Thomas Berry. Reprinted with permission of Sierra Club Books.

Berry, Wendell. Excerpt from "A Native Hill" from *Recollected Essays 1965–1980* by Wendell Berry. Copyright © 1981 by Wendell Berry. Reprinted by permission of North Point Press, a division of Farrar, Straus and Giroux, LLC. "To Know the Dark" from *The Selected Poems of Wendell Berry* by Wendell Berry. Copyright © 1998 by Wendell Berry. Reprinted by permission of Counterpoint Press, a member of Perseus Books, L.L.C. "'The Farm' IX" from *A Timbered Choir* by Wendell Berry. Copyright © 1998 by Wendell Berry. Reprinted by permission of Counterpoint Press, a member of Perseus Books, L.L.C. "The Peace of Wild Things" excerpted from: *Openings*. Copyright © 1968 by Wendell Berry. Published by Harcourt Brace. Reprinted with permission of the author.

Billings, Judith. "Lie quietly along the earth . . ." Copyright © 1999 by Judith Billings. From *Prayers for a Thousand Years* published by HarperSanFrancisco, edited by Elizabeth Roberts & Elias Amidon. Reprinted by permission of the author.

Buber, Martin. *The Life of the Hasidism* or *Tales of the Hasidim*. Copyright © 1947 by Martin Buber. Reprinted by permission of Random House, Inc.

Thein Durning. Reprinted by permission of Sasquatch Books.

Ehrlich, Gretel. "On Water," from *The Solace of Open Spaces* by Gretel Ehrlich, copyright © 1985 by Gretel Ehrlich. Used by permission of Viking Penguin, a division of Penguin Putnam Inc.

Eiseley, Loren. Excerpt from "The Star Thrower" in *The Unexpected Universe*. Copyright © 1969 by Loren Eiseley and renewed 1997 by John A. Eichman, III. Reprinted by permission of Harcourt, Inc. From the *Lost Notebooks of Loren Eiseley* by Kenneth Hewer. Copyright © 1987 by the Estate of Mabel L. Eiseley (unpublished Loren Eiseley material): copyright © 1987 by Kenneth Hewer (edited intro, reminiscence conclusion, notes, and captions). By permission of Little, Brown and Company (Inc.). From *The Immense Journey* by Loren Eiseley. Copyright © 1953 by Loren Eiseley. Published by Time, Inc. Reprinted by permission of Random House, Inc.

Evans, Bruce A. and Raynold Gideon. From the motion picture *Starman*, written by Bruce A. Evans and Raynold Gideon. Courtesy of Columbia Pictures.

Finch, Robert. From *Outlands* by Robert Finch. Reprinted by permission of David R. Godine, Publisher, Inc. Copyright © 1986 by Robert Finch.

Frank, Anne. From *The Diary of Anne Frank: The Critical Edition* by Anne Frank. Copyright © 1986 by Anne Frank-Fonds, Basle/Switzerland, for all texts of Anne

Frank. Used by permission of Doubleday, a division of Random House, Inc.

Galvan, Michael. From *Faith and Cultures: A Multicultural Catechetical Resource* by Michael Galvan. Published by the United States Catholic Conference. Permission to reprint courtesy of the author.

Gerber, Dan. "Walking in Tierra del Fuego" from *Sacred Trusts: Essays on Stewardship & Responsibility* © 1993 edited by Michael Katakis. Published by Mercury House, San Francisco, CA, and reprinted by permission.

Goethe, Johann Wolfgan von. 'Epirrhema' is taken from *Goethe: Roman Elegies and other Poems & Epigrams* translated by Michael Hamburger. Revised and expanded edition published by Anvil Press Poetry in 1996.

Gray, Elizabeth Dodson. "And the voice of God comes to us" by Elizabeth Dodson Gray. Copyright © 1999 by Elizabeth Dodson Gray. From *Prayers for a Thousand Years* published by HarperSanFrancisco, edited by Elizabeth Roberts & Elias Amidon. Reprinted by permission of Roundtable Press, Wellesley, MA. From *Green Pardise Lost* by Elizabeth Dodson Gray. Copyright © 1979 by Elizabeth Dodson Gray. Reprinted by permission of Roundtable Press, Wellesley, MA.

Haines, John. Excerpts from *The Stars, the Snow, the Fire* by John Haines. Copyright © 1989, 2000 by John Haines. Reprinted with the permission of Graywolf Press, Saint Paul, Minnesota.

Hay, John. From *The Undiscovered Country* by John Hay. Copyright © 1981 by John Hay. Used by permission of W. W. Norton & Company, Inc. Reprinted by permission of Sterling Lord Literistic, Inc. Copyright by John Hay.

Hermann, Hesse. From Hermann Hesse, Stunden in Garten. Gesammette Schriften in 7 Bänden, Band V. © Suhrkamp Verlag Frankfurt am Main 1957.

Hoagland, Edward. *"Thoughts on Returning to the City After Five Months on a Mountain"* from *Red Wolves and Black Bears* by Edward Hoagland. Published by Lyons & Burford. Originally appeared in *The Village Voice*. Copyright © 1972, 1976, 1995 by Edward Hoagland. This usage granted by permission of Lescher & Lescher, Ltd.

Hogan, Linda. From *Dwellings: A Spriritual History of the Living World* by Linda Hogan. Copyright © 1995 by Linda Hogan. Used by permission of W. W. Norton & Company, Inc.

Homer, Athanassakis. *The Homeric Hymns*. pp. 67, hymn 30. Copyright © 1976 by The Johns Hopkins University Press.

Hubbell, Sue. From *A Country Year: Living the Questions* by Sue Hubbell. Copyright © 1986 by Sue Hubbell. Published by Random House. Permission to reprint by Darhansoff and Verill Literary Agency.

Hughes, Langston. "Dream Variations" from *Collected Poems* by Langston Hughes. Copyright © 1994 by the

Estate of Langston Hughes. Reprinted by permission
of Alfred A. Knopf, a Division of Random House, Inc.

Hughes, Ted. All lines from "The Bear" from *Wodwo*
by Ted Hughes. Copyright © 1966 by Ted Hughes.
Reprinted by permission of HarperCollins Publishers, Inc.

Hurston, Zora Neale. From Chapter 27 of *Seraph on
the Suwanee,* by Zora Neale Hurston.
Copyright © 1948 by Zora Neale Hurston.
Published by Charles Scribner's Sons.

Kingsolver, Barbara. Excerpts, as submitted, from
The Poisonwood Bible by Barbara Kingsolver.
Copyright © 1998 by Barbara Kingsolver. Reprinted
by permission of HarperCollins Publishers, Inc.

Lame Deer. Reprinted with the permission of Pocket
Books, a division of Simon & Schuster from *Lame Deer
Seeker of Visions* by John Fire/Lame Deer and Richard
Erdoes. Copyright © 1972 by John Fire/Lame Deer and
Richard Erdoes.

Lawrence, D. H. "A Doe at Evening" published in
Animals Poems, selected and edited by John Hollander,
Everyman's Library Pocket Poets, Alfred A. Knopf/
David Campbell Publishers Ltd. Penguin USA.
Copyright © 1994.

Lennon, John and Paul McCartney. *Blackbird* words and
music by John Lennon and Paul McCartney. Copyright
© 1968 Sony/ATV Songs LLC (renewed). All rights
administered by Sony/ATV Music Publishing, 8 Music

Leopold, Aldo. From *A Sand County Almanac: And Sketches Here and There* by Aldo Leopold. Copyright © 1949, 1977 by Oxford University Press, Inc. Used by permission of Oxford University Press, Inc.

Levertov, Denise. "Come Into Animal Presence" by Denise Levertov, from *Poems 1960–1967.* Copyright © 1966 by Denise Levertov. Reprinted by permission of New Directions Publishing Corp.

Li Po. From "The Poetry and Career of Li Po" by Arthur Waley. Copyright © 1950 by Arthur Waley. Published by Geo. Allen & Unwin, Ldn. Macmillan Corp. N.Y. Reprinted by permission of John Robinson, copyright holder to the Arthur Waley Estate.

Lopez, Barry. Excerpts, as submitted, from *Crossing Open Ground* and *Arctic Dreams* by Barry Lopez. Reprinted by permission of Sterling Lord Literistic, Inc. Copyright © 1986 by Barry Lopez.

Marshall, Peter. From *Nature's Web: Rethinking Our Place on Earth* by Peter Marshall. Copyright © 1994 by Peter Marshall. Reprinted by permission from Paragon House.

Matthiessen, Peter. From *The Cloud Forest* by Peter Matthiessen. Copyright © 1961 by Peter Matthiessen. Used by permission of Viking Penguin, a division of Penguin Putnam Inc.

Maclean, Norman. From *A River Runs Through It* by
Norman Maclean. Copyright © 1976 by The University
of Chicago. Copyright © 1989 by Pennyroyal Press, Inc.,
All rights reserved. Originally published in 1976.
Published by The University of Chicago Press. Reprinted
by permission of The University of Chicago Press.

McPhee, Jack. From *Wanamurraganya: The Story of Jack
McPhee* by Sally Morgan, Fremantle Arts Centre Press,
Western Australia, 1989.

Meade, Erica Helm. "Dance of the Deer" from *Intimate
Nature* by Brenda Peterson, Deena Metzger, and Linda
Hogan. Copyright © 1998 by Brenda Peterson, Deena
Metzger, and Linda Hogan. Reprinted by permission of
Ballantine Books, a Division of Random House, Inc.

Mercer, Johnny. "Come Rain or Shine," words by
Johnny Mercer. Copyright © 1946. All rights reserved.
Permission to reprint by Hal Leonard Corporation.

Merton, Thomas. "Rain and the Rhinocerous" by
Thomas Merton from *Raids on the Unspeakable.*Copyright
© 1966 by The Abbey of Gethsemani, Inc. Reprinted by
permission of New Directions Publishing Corp.

Metzger, Deena. "God, in Your form of Beauty be with
us" by Deena Metzger. Copyright © 1999 by Deena
Metzger. From *Prayers for a Thousand Years* published by
HarperSanFrancisco, edited by Elizabeth Roberts &
Elias Amidon. Reprinted by permission of the author.

O'Connor, Flannery. Excerpt from "The King of Birds" from *Mystery and Manners* by Flannery O'Connor. Copyright © 1969 by the estate of Mary Flannery O'Connor. Reprinted by permission of Farrar, Straus and Giroux, LLC and Harold Matson Co., Inc.

Okakura, Kakuzo. From *The Book of Tea* by Kakuzo Okakura. Published by Kodansha International Ltd.

Okri, Ben. From *An African Elegy* by Ben Okri. Copyright © 1992. Jonathan Cape, publisher. Permission to reprint by The Random House Archive and Library, a division of the Random House Group Ltd.

Oliver, Mary. Excerpt from "Staying Alive" in *Blue Pastures*. Copyright © 1995, 1992, 1991 by Mary Oliver. Reprinted by permission of Harcourt, Inc.

Ortiz, Alphonso. "Look to the Mountaintop" by Alphonso Ortiz in *Essays in Reflection II*, edited by E. Graham Ward, et al. Copyright © 1973.

Orwell, George. "Some Thoughts on the Common Toad" from *Shooting an Elephant and Other Essays* by George Orwell. Copyright © 1946 by Sonia Brownell Orwell and renewed 1974 by Sonia Orwell. Reprinted by permission of Harcourt, Inc.

Perkins, Edna Brush. "The Feel of the Outdoors," from *The White Heart of Mojave: An Adventure with the Outdoors of the Desert*. Copyright © 1922, 1950. Reprinted by permission of Boni & Liveright Publishing Corporation.

Peters, Lenrie. "Autumn Burns Me" by Lenrie Peters first appeared in *Satellites*. Permission to reprint granted by the author.

Piercy, Marge. "Crows" from *Circles on the Water* by Marge Piercy. Copyright © 1982 by Marge Piercy. Reprinted by permission of Alfred A. Knopf, a Division of Random House, Inc.

Rawlings, Marjorie Kinnan. Excerpt from *Cross Creek* by Marjorie Kinnan Rawlings. Copyright © 1942 by Marjorie Kinnan Rawlings. Copyright renewed © 1970 Norton Baskin. Reprinted by permission of Brandt & Brandt Literary Agents, Inc.

Reben, Martha. Excerpt from "Night Song" from *A Sharing of Joy* by Martha Reben. Published in 1963 by Harcourt, Inc.

Richmond, Lewis. From *Work as a Spiritual Practice: A Practical Buddhist Approach to Inner Growth and Satisfaction on the Job* by Lewis Richmond. Copyright © 1999. Permission to reprint by Broadway Books, a division of Random House, Inc.

Rilke, Rainer Maria. "Ich lebe mein Leben…/I live my life in widening," "Da neight sich die Stunde…/The hour is striking," from *Rilke's Book of Hours: Love Poems To God* by Rainer Maria Rilke, translated by Anita Barrows and Joanna Macy. Copyright © 1996 by Anita Barrows and Joanna Macy. Used by permission of Riverhead Books, a division of Penguin Putnam, Inc.

Sandburg, Carl. Excerpt from "Moonlight and Maggots" in *The Complete Poems of Carl Sandburg*. Copyright © 1970, 1969 by Lilian Steichen Sandburg, Trustee. Reprinted by permission of Harcourt, Inc.

Sanders, Scott Russell. From *Staying Put* by Scott Russell Sanders. Copyright © 1993 by Scott Russell Sanders. Reprinted by permission of Beacon Press, Boston. From *Secrets of the Universe* by Scott Russell Sanders. Copyright © 1991 Scott Russell Sanders. Reprinted by permission of Beacon Press, Boston.

Sappho. "Leave Krete and Come to This Holy Temple" from *Sappho and the Greek Lyric Poets* by Willis Barnstone, translator. Copyright © 1962, 1967, 1988 by Willis Barnstone. Reprinted by permission of Schocken Books, a division of Random House, Inc.

Schweitzer, Albert. Excerpts, as submitted, from *Reverence for Life: The Words of Albert Schweitzer* by Albert Schweitzer. Collection copyright © 1993 by Harold Robles. Foreword copyright © 1993 by Rhena Schweitzer Miller. Reprinted by permission of HarperCollins Publishers, Inc.

Seton, Julia M. "Prologue" from *By a Thousand Fires* by Julia M. Seton. Copyright © 1967. Published by Doubleday. Permission to reprint by Doubleday, a division of Random House, Inc.

Seton-Thompson, Grace. "Windows of the Soul," Stanza 9 from *The Singing Traveler* by Grace Seton-Thompson. Copyright 1947. Published by Doubleday.

Suzuki. D. T. "Introduction" by D. T. Suzuki from
Zen in the Art of Archery by Eugen Herrigel. Copyright
© 1953, 1971. Published by Pantheon and Vintage.
Reprinted by permission of Random House, Inc.

Taggard, Genevieve. "Demeter" from *Slow Music*
by Genevieve Taggard. Published by Harper & Bros.,
New York. Copyright © 1946 by Genevieve Taggard.
Permission to reprint by Marcia D. Liles.

Trimble, Stephen. From *Geography of Childhood* by Gary
Paul Nabhan and Stephen Trimble. Copyright © 1994
by Gary Paul Nabhan and Stephen Trimble. Reprinted
by permission of Beacon Press, Boston.

Turner, Jack. From *Abstract Wild,* by Jack Turner.
Copyright © 1996 John S. Turner. Reprinted by
permission of the University of Arizona Press.

Uvavnuk. "The great sea has sent me adrift" by
Uvavnuk in *The Intellectual Life of the Iglulik Eskimos* by
Knut Rasmussen, trans. from the Danish by W. E.
Calvert, 1930.

Wagoner, David. "Lost" from *Traveling Light*. Copyright
© 1999 by David Wagoner. Used with permission of
the Poet and the University of Illinois Press.

Wallace, David Rains. From *The Klamath Knot:
Explorations of Myth and Evolution* by David Rains
Wallace. Copyright © 1983 by David Rains Wallace.
Reprinted with permission of Sierra Club Books.

SELECTED BIBLIOGRAPHY

Beyond those titles mentioned in the acknowledgments, these volumes were essential source material. Jason Gardner's *The Sacred Earth: Writers on Nature and Spirit* and Timothy Freke's *The Illustrated Book of Sacred Scriptures* deserve special mention and gratitude for their refined utility.

Anderson, Lorraine, ed. *Sisters of the Earth: Women's Prose and Poetry about Nature*. New York: Vintage Books, A Division of Random House, 1991.

Barnhill, David Landis, ed. *At Home on the Earth: Becoming Native to Our Place, A Multicultural Anthology*. Berkeley: University of California Press, 1999.

Bernbaum, Edwin. *Sacred Mountains of the World*. San Francisco: Sierra Club Books, 1990.

Dunn, Sara with Alan Scholefield. *Poetry for the Earth*. New York: Fawcett Columbine, 1991.

Farrell, Kate, ed. *Art & Nature: An Illustrated Anthology of Nature Poetry*. New York: The Metropolitan Museum of Art, 1992.

Finch, Robert and John Elder, eds. *The Norton Book of Nature Writing*. New York: W. W. Norton & Company, 1990.

Freke, Timothy. *The Illustrated Book of Sacred Scriptures*. Wheaton, Illinois: Quest Books, Theosophical Publishing House, 1998.

Gardner, Jason, ed. *The Sacred Earth: Writers on Nature and Spirit*. Novato, California: New World Library, 1998.

Harvey, Andrew and Anne Baring, comps. *The Mystic Vision: Daily Encounters with the Divine*. San Francisco: HarperSanFrancisco, 1995.

Hogan, Linda, Deena Metzger, and Brenda Peterson, eds. *Intimate Nature: The Bond Between Women and Animals*. New York: Fawcett Books, The Ballantine Publishing Group, 1998.

Hollander, John, ed. *Animal Poems*. Everyman's Library Pocket Poets. New York: Alfred A. Knopf, 1994.

The Holy Bible, King James' Version. Philadelphia: A. J. Holman Company, 1924.

McLuhan, T. C., *The Way of the Earth: Encounters with Nature in Ancient and Contemporary Thought*. New York: Simon & Schuster, 1994.

Partington, Angela, ed. *The Concise Oxford Dictionary of Quotations*. Oxford: Oxford University Press, 1997.

Partnow, Elaine, ed. *The Quotable Woman: An Encyclopedia of Useful Quotations Indexed by Subject & Author, 1800–On*. Garden City, New York: Anchor Books, Anchor Press/Doubleday, 1978.

Princeton Language Institute, The, ed. *21st Century Dictionary of Quotations*. Produced by the Philip Lief Group Inc. New York: A Laurel Book, Dell Publishing, a division of Bantam Doubleday Dell Publishing Group, Inc., 1993.

Roberts, Elizabeth and Elias Amidon, eds. *Prayers for a Thousand Years: Blessings and Expressions of Hope for the New Millennium*. San Francisco: HarperSanFrancisco, 1999.

Scharper, Stephen B. and Hilary Cunningham, comps. and eds. *The Green Bible*, Maryknoll, New York: Orbis Books, 1993.

Stone, Jana, ed. *Every Part of This Earth Is Sacred: Native American Voices in Praise of Nature*. San Francisco: HarperSanFrancisco, 1993.

Trimble, Stephen, ed. *Words from the Land: Encounters with Natural History Writing*. Expanded ed. Reno: University of Nevada Press, 1995.

INDEX OF AUTHORS